What Jewish Schools Could Be

THE VIEW FROM THE OTHER SIDE

by
Sara Carter

Mazo Publishers

What Jewish Schools Could Be
ISBN: 978-1-936778-90-4

Copyright © 2011 by Sara Carter
Email: saraccrtr@yahoo.com

Published by:
Mazo Publishers

P.O. Box 10474
Jacksonville, FL 32247 USA
1-815-301-3559

P.O. Box 36084
Jerusalem 91360 Israel
054-7294-565

Website: www.mazopublishers.com
Email: cm@mazopublishers.com

Book production by
Prestige PrePress
Email: prestige.prepress@gmail.com

Cover image
Werner Münzker | Dreamstime.com

All rights reserved.
No part of this publication may be translated, reproduced, stored in a retrieval system, or transmitted in any form or by any means, electronic, mechanical, photocopying, recording or otherwise, without prior permission in writing from the publisher.

"Blessed are You,

Lord our G-d,

King of the Universe,

Who gives the rooster understanding

To distinguish between day and night."

Morning Blessings, Siddur

Contents

About The Author		7
Rationale For This Book		8
Preface		10
1	Breaking The Habit Of Surrendering To Labels	22
2	Avoiding a March through the Curriculum with a Prescribed One-Size-Fits-All Method	49
3	Confronting the Harmful Consequences of the Present Uses of Testing	80
4	Putting It All Together to Nurture a Paradigm Shift	106
5	Words of Encouragement	133
References		139
Other Resources		142
Acknowledgments		143

About The Author

Sara Carter began her teaching career as one of two teachers who started the Children's School, grades 1-8, in Atlanta, Georgia. Later she taught for over fifteen years at the Chaya Mushka Children's House, a Jewish Montessori school, where she mentored teachers and obtained state licensing and national accreditation for this school. She has conducted workshops at regional educational conferences and is presently a consultant at the Intown Jewish Preschool in Atlanta.

Sara is a song composer and also an accomplished musician. She has developed and taught music programs.

Sara graduated as valedictorian from Newcomb College of Tulane University and was awarded a Woodrow Wilson Fellowship. She earned an M.A. degree from the University of California at Berkeley and an M.A. in Teaching from Emory University in Atlanta, where she currently lives.

Rationale For This Book

From her earliest years in public school, Sara Carter learned easily. In all subjects she excelled with a minimum of effort. Homework was finished quickly, and she continued down the path toward becoming and remaining a straight-A student, even through four years of undergraduate college. Her attribute of obedience led her to learn whatever was presented, and she gradually became expert at "reading" her teachers and returning to them exactly what they wanted to hear. Some time during her college years, she became aware that she was playing a game. She could write a beautiful critique of a poem or compose a thoughtful essay, but she had a nagging feeling that she was becoming a machine, an academically successful robot. "Hopefully," she thought, "in graduate school I'll be able to think. I'll be able to leave behind the well-established habit of doing what was necessary to make high grades and finally do some real learning." Alas, she entered an intensely competitive atmosphere where, again, she succeeded, but now the price was too high to pay. After completing her masters degree, she left the world of academia for a while.

Now that she did have time to think, Sara wondered, "How could this be? How could it be that my college roommate, who also made good grades, panicked in her senior year and asked

Rationale For This Book

me to help her study for an important final exam 'because,' she admitted, 'I don't know how to think!'? How could it be that most teachers taught their subjects, and either a student matched his way of thinking to the teacher's or he was unable to do so and was labeled below average or lacking in intelligence altogether? How could it be that I never saw a teacher working hard to help a student become greater than he was at the moment? Why is it that by the time many students finished school, they thought so little of themselves as learners?"

These were a few of the questions that led Sara back to college, this time to learn how to be a teacher and how to make it real. Once again, she saw that reaching this goal was not going to occur within the walls of a university. She obtained the graduate degree which would allow her to begin teaching, and the following twenty years became her laboratory for the real learning she had been seeking for so long. Wishing to share with others her accumulated insights from years of practice, study, and reflection, Sara wrote this book.

Preface

Avraham, the first Jew, was called *ivri* – the one on the other side. Imagine for a moment that we are standing with him "on the other side," freed from the untruths that cloud our world and weigh us down. While we are standing there, we could ask ourselves, "Are our Jewish schools everything they could be?" The answer would be clear: We have work to do. We need to remake our schools because we are losing our grasp on the good we want for our children. Within all the particular versions of this good lies the hope that our children will be sensitive, responsive human beings, eager to relate to others with confidence, with optimism, and with a Torah morality. Education, therefore, must be viewed as a type of meeting – with oneself, with a friend, with a teacher, with a subject, and with *Hashem*. To be sure, an educative moment defined as a meeting can happen anywhere, but my purpose here is to motivate people concerned with schools – teachers, administrators, and parents – to create classrooms filled with daily opportunities for meetings. A genuine meeting should leave me with the sense that I am no longer the same. In a small way or in a profound way, my customary frameworks should now appear inadequate. I should be dissatisfied with today, and brave enough to move into tomorrow.

Preface

We would all agree that without water, food, and shelter, a person cannot safeguard his body. We spend much of our time taking care of our material needs, and rightfully so, but in the process, we tend to lose sight of the fact that without a meeting, without a sense of connection, a person cannot nourish his uniqueness as a human. Even with water, food, and shelter, a person can become so isolated that he sees neither a past nor a future for himself. For a Jew, a lack of connection of this magnitude could be a way of describing the worst possible exile. What, after all, is exile? It is a separation from the voice of our *neshama,* our soul.

Thankfully, most of us don't suffer from this extreme form of exile; nevertheless, our energies are drained by the reality of twenty-first century life as a collection of out-of-sync experiences. From our human perspective, the parts don't seem to mesh together to make a wholesome, coherent progression. News and opinions assault us in a highly disjointed fashion, leaving us wondering whether we can participate in a rational discussion of anything. Aware parents try their best to make the pieces of their lives fit together in some kind of harmony for their children, but this effort requires constant thoughtfulness and vigilance. Our greatest present need in education is a similar thoughtfulness and vigilance on the part of those who work in our schools.

Educators need to schedule regular times for reviewing what they are doing in the light of their vision of the end result. If this end result is a Jew who has a keen awareness of his soul and of the power he has to reveal G-dliness in the material world, then his education will proceed to show him the connection to be made between his soul and his actions. It will encourage a sustained connection in the form of thriving relationships among his peers, among his teachers, between himself and his teachers, and between himself and his studies – a kind of "harmony in progress."

Without this connective tissue, some learning will occur, but it will not be optimal. All of us have met a number of students who seem to be able to learn under almost any circumstances; however, we forget to reckon the costs they have unnecessarily paid. We also squirm with the knowledge that a far greater number of students lose out unnecessarily. Not only is their learning minimal, they also succumb to a negative attitude towards themselves and their ability to be a part of the learning community. Obviously this development has a negative impact on their emotional and social well-being and on the health of the entire Jewish people.

Those who are good at nurturing children have always understood the importance of connection. In the past few years, scientists who are conducting research on brain and child development are acknowledging the primary significance of a human being's need for connection. Connectedness is the centerpiece of a stunning report produced in 2003 by a thirty-three member Commission on Children at Risk.[1] Their report originated from a concern about the growing deterioration of children's mental and emotional health in the USA. It states that the human child is biologically primed to connect to others, to moral and spiritual meaning, and to transcendence. The Commission concluded that meeting these needs for connection is essential for mental and emotional health and for human flourishing. (More details about this report appear in Chapter 1.)

Through the healthy interplay between an infant and his primary caregivers, the human being begins to lay the foundation for future connections. When he becomes a student, his continued growth and well-being will be predicated, in large part, on the degree to which he can depend on his school for the connections he needs. If his school values connections, he will be far more likely to internalize his learning and to apply it in novel situations rather than to place his learning in a theoretical box with no relation to his everyday living. He will also be far more likely to sense the unity of the Jewish people, not just as a proclamation but as a reality. Thus, you will find throughout this book a recurring emphasis on connection. If we can design an environment that prioritizes this vital element of existence, we can be confident that we are on the path to the lofty, but attainable, goal of refinement of the self and refinement of our world.

Apparently, Jewish schools which live with

---

[1] *Hardwired to Connect: The New Scientific Case for Authoritative Communities.*

this goal and safeguard it on a daily basis are rare. We and our institutions are vulnerable to societal pressures that gradually push us off our chosen path. As a result, too many of our teachers and principals become caught in unproductive practices which, when examined, are found to be inconsistent with Torah values. Practices like labeling students, pushing them through curricula with very little concern for understanding and application, and reinforcing our society's wholesale adoption of tests and competition as the way to motivate learning do have an effect on our children. For example, after being told that *ahavas Yisroel* is the fundamental mitzvah of the Torah, students become perplexed when they sense that an all-embracing commitment to this mitzvah is lacking in their school. Younger children most probably feel a generalized discomfort stemming from this inconsistency; even older students may not find it easy to articulate their dissatisfaction or to discover why this mitzvah is not more fully expressed. The reality is that labeling, rushing through curricula, and emphasizing testing are practices which erode the growth of *ahavas Yisroel*. Even graver than this outcome are the indirect messages these practices send. They are telling our children that externalities define a person, that success is measured by comparison to others, that individual success is to be prized over the cultivation of empathy and community, that the inner life, since it cannot be measured, has little value. Even worse, many of our children become unaware that they have an inner dimension to themselves that is worthy of their

Preface

attention. This less than desirable situation has serious repercussions; teachers themselves suffer from a loss of their own humanity, and they watch as many of their students become more troubled, angry, petty, and mean.

This book is my attempt to help us reclaim the original purpose of a Jewish school and to ensure that our actions will remain connected to this purpose. Teachers and principals would, no doubt, tell me that they are eager to embrace the kind of school that empowers their students to be active partners with *Hashem* in the perfection of our world. Such educators begin their careers with the serious intention of enhancing their own humanity and that of their students. Above all, they intend to show their students the greatness of the Torah and the joy of being a Jew.

Children begin their lives at school filled with curiosity and a desire to express their delight with the world and to ask their endless questions. Their powerful, innate drive to learn is evident in their every move. They are even eager, at first, for homework, which they interpret as a sign of being older and more capable. They are also working hard at learning how to operate in a world filled with others. All of these explorations reflect their need to make meaning out of their experiences. Not only students but all of us need time for this kind of internal activity.

As a student moves through the grades, however, the time for making meaning and the guidance which may assist it become less and less available. Eagerness, delight, attachment – these begin to take a back seat. I once overheard a bright boy of middle-school age make the following comment: "Kindergarten is okay – even first and second grade, but after that it's all downhill." How can we afford to ignore his opinion? He may have learned to lower his expectations drastically; it is, after all, a way of coping. Must we, as responsible adults, likewise learn to settle for less? Obviously not. We must learn to listen to our students and to comprehend why they would describe their journey through school as a downhill one.

One possible understanding of this middle-school boy is that he is reacting to a dehumanizing effect that afflicts both himself and his teachers. The longer one stays in most schools, the more he feels himself becoming a nonentity. The welcoming smile of a teacher and the cheerful "good morning" are not enough to take away the feeling that slowly one's identity is being submerged in the relentless movement through classes that speak to some theoretical, generalized student who has very little resemblance to himself.

Donna Goertz, an accomplished teacher in Austin, Texas, gives us a graphic description of this process. She writes that most school environments are designed "to produce students of a predetermined proficiency in a pre-set curriculum laid out in an incrementally programmed time sequence, as well as a predetermined schedule of expectations of achievement..."[2] Experts in education have seen how this design harms many students; it is no less

---

2   Goertz, 2001, 224.

than a daily dose of alienation from oneself.

We need to face the harmfulness of this design; otherwise, we will continue to tinker with the present structure, all the while subjecting teachers and students to more and more pressure, a pressure that comes in many guises, all of which subtly rob teachers and students of their integrity. Too often their lives at school become a kind of game in which honesty and truthfulness are compromised. They are left spending far too much of their energy simply coping – either with humor, resignation, disruptive activity, or withdrawal. Because too many of our present schools do not recognize "the reality of the child as a naturally driven learner,"[3] they come to rely too much on external motivations such as rewards and punishments and a thoughtless acceptance of competition that isolates students from each other. It is no wonder that teachers become discouraged and students become unable to empathize and to collaborate. Jewish teachers and students, in particular, suffer from conditions which do not allow the expression of their innate capacity for loving-kindness.[4]

When an educator becomes willing to face a problem as serious as this one, almost overwhelming in its ramifications, he should attach himself to two principles found in the Torah. One is that if a person finds himself in a position to see something that needs to be repaired, his being in this position is no accident. By Divine Providence he has been

---

3   Ibid., 223.
4   For a statement of this innate characteristic of a Jew, see *Yevamos* 79a.

brought to this vantage point; therefore, he has an ability to do something positive regarding the situation he sees.

The other principle is that a person should not tackle a large problem alone. He needs to find others who share his concerns and learn from their insights and the changes they are making. For many years I have looked for such people and have found a number of them. They all refuse to give up the idea that schools can actually be places where individuals can stay in touch with themselves, can learn in cooperation with others, can become stronger and stronger in the abilities with which they were blessed, and can strive to fulfill the intention of their Creator to be moral beings. The work of these people has strengthened my conviction that the desire for optimal learning environments in Jewish schools is a valid one. Especially now, the possibility of creating such environments is within our reach. We have access to a growing body of research describing how students learn best and a growing number of schools that are already successfully applying this knowledge. As you will notice, the findings from secular research and the resulting practices, though not stemming from a Torah perspective, have much in common with the eternal truths of the Torah.

A word is needed about my use of secular sources in a book whose ultimate frame of reference is the Torah. The Torah, as the will and wisdom of *Hashem*, lacks nothing; therefore, it is not the Torah that needs help. It is we human beings who need help in discovering the concrete actions for education that are implied in the Torah. For example, if the Torah insists upon the dignity and unique purpose of every Jew, then a teacher has to own these truths, fire his imagination, and change himself and his classroom with a moderate, step-by-step approach that keeps everyone's feet on the ground but moves with assurance toward these truths. It is here that we can benefit from secular contributions to education. Most of us need samples of good work in order to stimulate our imagination. I view the findings from recent research on the learning process and the practical application of these findings as just such samples. The question to be asked of this research is simple: Does our study of it improve our ability to see what the Torah wants us to do? The work of the educators I have included in this book does just that. Their writings are powerful stimuli for our imaginations. When an educator studies these writings, he will suddenly see, in a way not previously experienced, how to translate Torah wisdom into deed.

Rabbi Yitzchak Ginsburgh, author of numerous books on Torah subjects, including *The Art of Education*, offers the following perspective on the proper relationship between secular knowledge and Torah wisdom: "In general, Judaism relates positively to secular science and inquiry – as long as they seek to complement and enhance the wisdom of the Torah rather than to supplant or undermine it. Conversely, the wisdom of the Torah can identify what is true and what is not in secular inquiry, and associate each truth with its appropriate context in the Torah's own world-view."⁵ These words have encouraged me to consult sources from both worlds that will help to create optimal learning environments.

If we want such environments for our children, we must eliminate practices which dehumanize us and replace them with life-building ones. I have identified three practices which stand in the way of optimal learning environments: labeling, marching through curricula with little regard for understanding, and pervasive testing that distorts teaching and learning. I ask you to examine these practices with me so that we will be willing to leave them behind and move on to implement much-needed alternatives. The rationale for this book, then, is to arouse within us the courage and the determination to adopt practices that display the Torah's wisdom in every detail of our classrooms. The effort to create such classrooms is nothing less than the effort to regain the view from the other side.

---

5   Ginsburgh, 2002, footnote 18, 159.

What Jewish Schools Could Be

THE VIEW FROM THE OTHER SIDE

1
Breaking The Habit Of Surrendering To Labels

We put labels on the outside of objects like file cabinets and jars of home-made preserves so that we can quickly know what is on the inside. This labeling is not problematic. Labeling children is, because there is no way we can quickly know what is on the inside of a human being. Not only that, the inside of a human being is always changing. The preserves might be finished, but you and I are not.

The problem is exacerbated by the tendency of a label to gain a life of its own. In spite of our efforts to the contrary, we let the label become the definition of a person; we treat the label as a kind of conclusive description; therefore, we feel no need to explore any further who this person may be. We act as if we already know. Even worse, the person we have labeled may accept our perception of him as an accurate description.

The best that can be said for labels, e.g., "defiant," "confrontational," "impulsive," "bossy," and even "wheel-chair bound," is that they are mere points in the beginning of the unfolding of a person. They are signposts saying, "Invest in me. I need your help." Ironically, labels like "sweet," "bright," and "cooperative" may be the hardest to peel away; since such students are not likely to cause trouble, many teachers conclude that the needs of these students are being met.

One could argue, however, that labeling a child might be helpful. Wouldn't it be good to know that a certain student cannot understand numbers and, therefore, cannot tell time or figure out the correct change? (This difficulty has become a "condition" with a name – *dyscalculia*.) Committed teachers could help this student compensate and also let his peers know that though he has difficulty with numbers, he is quite competent in other areas and may have an outstanding talent. He may also be encouraged to advocate for himself by letting teachers know right away when he does not understand.

The hurtful part is that the student himself may decide not to explore any further the world of numbers and may avoid contexts in which he could, perhaps, make a break-through. Similarly, his teachers may give up instead of seeking alternative approaches. Once teachers accept that a student has a condition, two distortions in their thinking are likely to follow: they perceive the condition to be permanent, and they decide that the problem lies within the child and not within his environment. This line of thought leads to the next step – a casting off of responsibility. For example, once a teacher decides, even tentatively, that a child is hyperactive, the teacher will rarely ask the question, "Are the demands I am putting on this student, the assignments that I give, the way I structure the class, part of this child's problem?" And what about his home life and family history? I admit that these questions are likely to cause a teacher anxiety, and justifiably so, given the present parameters within which most of us work. Most teachers have little control over these parameters (curricula to cover, standardized tests to give, topics and materials to be used that were not chosen with teacher input, and a tremendous time squeeze because of the dual curriculum, just to name a few). In this kind of environment, it is not surprising that a teacher will begin to look upon the possibly hyperactive child as someone who is unable to succeed in a regular classroom.

If the school's discipline program has proven to be ineffective with this child, the teacher will usually request that the child be observed by a specialist. The specialist may give the teacher specific changes to be made within the classroom and/or may recommend that the child be tested for some type of disorder or disability. Depending on the ability of the teacher to make the suggested changes and / or the quality of the testing experience, a diagnosis may follow that, with more and more frequency, leads to medication.

Now we are at a problematic moment: the child has been labeled, but this label has described only a collection of symptoms and has not addressed underlying causes. (We haven't learned what is on the inside. We don't even know if the child has a true illness.) Secondly, the responsibility for changing into a more cooperative, settled child is now placed, for the most part, on the medication, not on the child's teachers or the environment that defines his school. Even so, one could hope that if a reasonable amount of psychotherapy could be obtained in conjunction with the medication, the child and his parents and teachers might gain some understanding. What usually happens, however, is that managed care or other insurance programs may not pay for enough visits; there is immense pressure on the psychotherapist to provide a "quick fix." Parents are also being pressured to give their children medication in order to ease problems of classroom management. This approach to problems assumes that it is the child who must adjust to the school. A child on medication appears to have met this demand. Principals and teachers, therefore, may consider themselves absolved from the effort to rethink how best to meet the needs of their students. In the meantime, the child may well be taking a drug for a condition that he does not have.

George Halasz, an Australian child and adolescent psychiatrist, and four of his colleagues have put together a small book entitled *Cries Unheard*, published in 2002. In this book they carefully describe these and other alarming developments in the mental health-care field, especially with regards to attention deficit hyperactivity disorder (ADHD). Two of their main points have to do with the astounding proliferation of labels of mental illness and the extraordinary increase in the numbers of children taking Ritalin. Dr. Halasz quotes H. Redner's observation that the Diagnostic and Statistical Manual of Mental Disorders "listed a mere 60 illnesses in 1952; this grew to 145 in 1968 and in 1994 stood at 410, with strong potential for further growth." Redner emphasizes, "Particularly badly affected by this constantly creeping diagnostic expansion have been children, whose least oddity or not quite normal (frequently confused with average) quirk is now assigned to some syndrome or other and treated with behavior therapy and drugs. The ethics of all this is rarely called into question."[1]

Regarding the numbers of children taking Ritalin, Anne Manne reports that from 1990 to 1998, the number of American children and adults diagnosed with ADHD jumped from about nine hundred thousand to almost five million. "This resulted in a seven hundred-fold increase in Ritalin production. Likewise, the numbers of children prescribed Prozac for depression quadrupled in the same period." She urges that we should "stop dead in our tracks and ponder why."[2]

At about the same time that Halasz and his colleagues were seeking explanations for the growing numbers of medicated children, a group of scientists and practitioners in the USA were confronting similar troubling data about America's youth. This group became the Commission on Children at Risk, mentioned earlier in the Preface.

1   Halasz, Anaf, Ellingsen, Manne, and Salo, 2002, 5.
2   Ibid., 8, 10. See also "The Attention Deficit Debacle," 7-8, *In Their Own Way* by Thomas Armstrong, 2000.

Sponsored in part by Dartmouth Medical School, the commission included leading children's doctors, neuroscientists, research scholars, and youth service professionals. The data they surveyed indicated that a large and growing number of children and young people in the USA are suffering from depression, anxiety, attention deficit, conduct disorders, thoughts of suicide, and other serious mental and behavioral problems. Their purpose was to find out why and what can be done to reverse this trend; the title of the resulting report is *Hardwired to Connect: The New Scientific Case for Authoritative Communities*.

The commission identified two crises. The first one is the downward trend in mental health just mentioned. The second one is "...how we as a society are thinking about this deterioration."[3] The commission suggests that our intellectual models are inadequate. We are presently focusing on individual pathology and dysfunction, which "...locates the problem as 'inside' the person, rather than as stemming at least partly from the environment." The report acknowledges that both approaches are necessary, but that today, we do not have the balance right. The commission urges us to broaden our attention to the environmental conditions creating growing numbers of suffering children.[4]

This focus on the environment came about as the commission reviewed a large body of scientific

---

3   *Hardwired to Connect*, 2003, 5.
4   Ibid., 14.

research which kept pointing to an intricate "dance," a back and forth movement of influence between nurturing environments on the one hand, and brain circuitry and even gene expression, on the other. The commission found a great deal of evidence, largely from the field of neuroscience, which shows that the human being is hardwired for close attachments to other people and is hardwired for making meaning. We are "...born with a built-in capacity and drive to search for purpose and reflect on life's ultimate ends. Meeting the human child's deep need for these related aspects of connectedness – to other people and to meaning – is essential to the child's health and development."[5]

The commission then states that the institutions which traditionally met the child's need for connectedness have become weakened to a significant degree. This weakening of what the commission calls "authoritative communities"[6] in the USA is the principal reason why so many of our children are failing to flourish. The report, therefore, recommends the renewal and strengthening of authoritative communities as the best strategy for improving the lives of our children and adolescents.

This recommendation pushes us away from the dominant pharmacological model and towards the

---

5   Ibid.
6   The commission defines authoritative communities as groups of people who are committed to one another over time and who model and pass on at least part of what it means to be a good person and live a good life. The report lists ten characteristics of any authoritative community.

prevention, or ecological, model. In this way, it gives educators the impetus to think less in terms of labels and more in terms of broader changes in classroom and school environments.

Principals and teachers now have available to them the thorough-going and compassionate work of panels like the Commission on Children at Risk. In addition, new publications on the urgent problems confronting Jewish youth are appearing regularly from rabbinical leaders. By not taking the time to investigate these resources and to reflect on them together with their peers, educators subject themselves to an unexamined repetition of ineffective practices. For example, in too many middle and high school Gemara classes, the prevailing methods of teaching are not working for a significant number of students. An element that appears to be missing is an interest in the student that leads to a strong bond between himself and his rebbe. This bond becomes a secure base to be used for engaging the student and building his character. Current secular literature on education has begun to recognize the centrality of this bonding process, but many of us know that this crucial element originated in the Torah. Its lack in Jewish schools, therefore, hurts even more. A related problem is that many Gemara rebbes seem to be limited to one teaching style. As a result, they begin to perceive students who cannot benefit from this style as youngsters who will never be adequate to the task. These students are quick to take note of their rebbes' perception of them; thus begins a painful period of time for both the students and their parents. For the students, hours of their time are wasted, and their hopes to have a portion in the Torah are diminished. For the parents, panic may ensue as they search, often without success, for a yeshiva better suited to their child. Much of this distress could be avoided if rebbes were working in an atmosphere of continuing investigation and reflection.

In *To Teach a Jew*, Rabbi Shmuel Yaakov Klein has a chapter entitled "Labels." He writes, "Today's *melamed* and *morah* are in danger of giving in to a new sort of pedagogic temptation – labeling." He continues that ever since the use of a growing list of labels has become a "professional" norm, "...teachers are prone to cite them [the labels] as magical exemptions from taking responsibility."[7] He adds, "Today even outstanding educators tend to consign the special student to the realm of non-achievement because the labels have categorized him as a child who belongs there."[8] Rabbi Klein's view is that "A teacher is morally bound to try to unearth what is troubling the child." He urges educators to "begin with the assumption that a child would not be negative without a just explanation ... All challenges are derived from something. Try to find out what it is. Do not throw labels around."[9]

Through studies and actual experiences in classrooms, we have learned that a person's ability to exercise his mind with hope and courage is tied to his emotional state. The following is an example

---
7   Klein, 2001, 178 ff.
8   Ibid., 179.
9   Ibid., 180 ff.

which shows the turn-around that occurred when someone was able to supply a missing element in a student's emotional makeup. The *Mashgiach* of Kamenitz relates that he once visited the Gateshead Yeshiva. At this yeshiva there was a young boy who didn't speak to anyone; no one could tell if he knew how to study Gemara. The *Mashgiach* was asked to help; he began by asking the boy if he would act as his chauffeur. The boy was eager to do so and drove the *Mashgiach* around for three hours. "I saw that he was completely normal. It seemed to me that all he lacked was a sense of belonging... On the third day, the boy's *Rosh Yeshiva* commented to me that he had already seen a change in the boy. 'He has a little color in his cheeks now!'" The *Mashgiach* eventually persuaded the boy's parents to let him come to *Eretz Yisroel* to study in the *Mashgiach's* yeshiva. As this boy arrived at Ben Gurion Airport, four students accompanied the *Mashgiach* to welcome him. "They broke out in a little dance in the reception area...," and even began to sing. The entire yeshiva student body had been alerted about the arrival of this boy, and there was much clamoring over who were going to be the lucky ones to have him as a roommate. This boy studied there for two years and "literally became a different person." Consider that all this change was coming from a boy who, earlier in his life, had been taken to numerous psychologists and whose parents had been told the situation was hopeless.[10]

---

10   *Impressions*, Vol. I, Issue 5, the Chofetz Chaim Heritage Foundation, 2003.

This example illustrates the fundamental importance of a sense of belonging and the power of affirming a person's worth rather than highlighting his incompetencies. The *Mashgiach* communicated his simple desire to be with this student for a few days. I would guess that the main impact of this request was realized indirectly, not even with words! The *Mashgiach* acted with him in a loving way; I would imagine he looked at him with loving eyes. Many of us have experienced how powerful this manner of communication can be. The message of worthiness continued to be delivered by a chorus of voices in Israel. The result was a young man who reconnected to his own voice and found a bridge not only to his fellow Jews but to the Torah as well.

Angeline Lillard, a researcher in developmental psychology, refers us to several studies which indicate that "…a positive emotional climate within a classroom has been shown to be the most powerful predictor of students' motivation to learn, … and happy moods are associated with more expansive and integrated thinking and learning, and with detecting global patterns…."[11]

One way of describing a good teacher, then, is that he makes a conscious choice to create a positive emotional climate in his classroom. As a friend of mine once said, any time you interact with someone, you are teaching him something, whether or not you want to or intend to. In the light of this reality, something as simple as expressing confidence in one's students or modeling how to use errors as a

---

11   Lillard, 2005, 4.

path to growth becomes an immeasurable aid to students' continued learning. A teacher can create a safe and predictable environment for taking risks, and he can radiate a quiet optimism. Finally, he can demonstrate that although he is eager to learn from his students, he has an obligation which they do not have. A teacher has the obligation of leadership, which means that he must introduce his students "...to a world larger than their own experiences and egos, a world that expands their personal boundaries and enlarges their sense of community."[12]

Daniel Goleman, author of *Social Intelligence*, writes, "Good teachers are like good parents. By offering a secure base, a teacher creates an environment that lets students' brains function at their best. That base becomes a safe haven, a zone of strength from which they can venture forth to explore, to master something new, to achieve."[13] Goleman continues, "...whenever teachers create an empathic and responsive environment, students not only improve in their grades and test scores – they become eager learners. Even one supportive adult at school can make a difference to a student."[14]

In other words, when a teacher offers security and acceptance, he creates a climate which empowers a student to leave the familiar and venture into the unknown. When a student arrives at this point, his teachers can consider themselves successful.

Take a moment to think of the times when your

---

12   Palmer, 1998, 120.
13   Goleman, 2006, 283.
14   Ibid., 284.

own creativity was able to flow without obstruction, when you were able to take risks and revise when necessary. What were the conditions surrounding these times? I would guess that your environment allowed you to make important decisions about your work and to contact others for needed advice or additional information. You probably had some control over the time allotted for the task, and you certainly had no fear of being ridiculed. You also may have been the one who decided who your audience, if any, would be.

Now imagine a typical classroom. Most of the time, options like the above are not available to students. I am not suggesting that students need all of these options all of the time, but if teachers begin to incorporate more of such opportunities into their lesson plans, I predict that they will see high-quality work that far exceeds their expectations. As a part of this process, the abilities, the concerns, and the passions of their students will become more transparent. Another step will have been taken to peel away the labels.

It is true that the hurried tone of a tightly-scheduled school day is not conducive to the peeling away of labels. As with any challenge, however, a teacher has to make a decision: Will I let the apparent difficulties rule, or will I commit myself to discovering a more concrete picture of each student as he lives in and out of school? If a teacher decides to make this commitment, he can be sure that his mind and heart will open up to possibilities that in the past he would not have imagined.

Perhaps one way to begin to develop this commitment is to remember events in one's early schooling in the light of revealing or diminishing personhood. One teacher shared this memory with me. I will call her Miriam. Miriam grew up in a middle-sized southern city and attended public school. In her seventh grade, she was taking a science test in a classroom where the desks were lined up in neat rows. Sitting near her was a quiet girl who lived in a more rural part of the school district and who seemed to be slow. Miriam remembers her as having a ready smile on her face, in spite of the fact that she most probably was not learning much of the science curriculum. During the test, Miriam pushed her answer sheet over so that this girl could copy it. Much to Miriam's surprise, at the end of the test time, the teacher passed out a little slip of paper for each student to sign, saying, "I have or have not helped someone on this test." Miriam wrote that she had helped someone. The teacher gently asked her not to do this again.

Now, many years later, Miriam is reflecting on what happened. She sees that the science teacher not only needed to help the slower girl but also could have turned this event into a mine of information about Miriam! She could have asked herself just one question: What can I learn about Miriam from the fact that she tried to help her classmate, albeit in an unacceptable way? Let us imagine the teacher musing, "Maybe Miriam is the kind of person who wants to help. Come to think of it, I never see her with any friends. Maybe, since she makes such good grades, she could be paired with someone in my class. Maybe there is something she could do for the school." If the teacher had started to think in this way, many possibilities might have opened up. As it was, nothing happened. Life went on. Miriam was obviously "bright," and the other girl was perceived to be "slow," and that was that. Miriam comments, "Being able actually to help didn't materialize until much later in my life, but had it started earlier, who knows where it could have led? I must admit that I was as unaware as the teacher of the possibilities of this event. It stayed with me, though, and somehow, in spite of the fact that we never became friends, I can still see the wide shape of my classmate's face, a sprinkle of freckles decorating her cheeks, and her resigned but good-natured smile. If I had to describe the lasting emotional tone of this experience, it would be one of silence, as if the sound had been turned off."

Suppose you have a student who has already been labeled with a problem. An example might be some kind of "social dysfunction disorder." Approach him from a different angle, one that has little bearing on the so-called disorder. You could engage him in an activity where you need help. The unstated message to him is that he is important to you and that he belongs. This suggestion comes from the story of the yeshiva student at Gateshead, mentioned previously. You also might search among his classmates for someone who would be willing to work with him on this or some other activity. Keep watching for small improvements in this student's behavior. When you think he is ready, give him responsibility for something important to the class. Tell his parents how he has changed at school and ask them if they have noticed any changes in his behavior at home. Sometimes just giving students time to confront a problem together and talk about it freely can help a fellow student escape his label. A teacher related to me the following story. (The children's names have been changed.) Once, as a beginning teacher, she was outside with her class of eight-year-olds. Suddenly a student named Margaret came up to her crying. It seems that another student, Bob, had hit her. A few other children were standing close by, listening. The teacher felt perplexed and dismayed because Bob had a habit of hurting other children and of lying much of the time. Nobody liked him. She also knew that his father worked for the United Nations in New York, so she began a rather weak discourse on how Bob's father was trying to help nations stop hurting each other, and that's what we have to do, too. "This approach was probably not going very far," continued the teacher. "Meanwhile, another girl named Tammy began quietly to cry. Bob looked at her with exasperation and asked, 'Why are you crying? I didn't hit you.' With tears spilling down her cheeks, Tammy answered, 'Because Margaret's my friend. I like her.' Then, looking straight into Bob's eyes, she added, 'And I like you, too.' There was dead silence. Everyone seemed to be caught in the glow of what had just happened. Bob's face completely changed. A smile began to appear, a smile mixed with shyness, a smile like we had never seen on his face. From that moment, Bob's behavior completely changed. He began to cooperate; he stopped lying; he and his classmates began to enjoy each other. A few weeks later, he broke his leg and had to stay home for a few days. On the day that he came back, his classmates crowded around and cheered him as if he were a hero returning from a great battle."

Let us back up a bit in this story and present the possibility that this teacher could have gone immediately into punishment mode. Then the children's discussion probably would not have occurred, and the moment for that great and unforgettable surprise would have been lost.

Vivian Gussin Paley treasures moments like this one. She is a master at using dialogue in the classroom as a way to develop herself and her students. In one of her books, *You Can't Say You Can't Play*, she explores with children in kindergarten through fifth grade the phenomenon of rejection. She establishes a rule, "You can't say you can't play," and asks children at all these grade levels to discuss it with her. The conversations are remarkable; even the older children recall their hurt at being left out in their younger days, and everyone wishes that such a rule had been established earlier. Paley observes, "...each time a cause for sadness is removed for even one child, the classroom seems nicer. And, by association, we all rise in stature."[15] How appropriate for the story of Bob's transformation! Paley makes everyone see that dialogue enables the participants to express

---

15   Paley, 1993, 95.

their ownership of problems and possible solutions. Designing classrooms that invite dialogue must become so important to teachers that even when they feel they are faltering (as the teacher felt in Bob's story), they will persist in developing an atmosphere of security and trust that will allow people to reveal their thoughts.

One way to enhance teacher-to-teacher and teacher-to-student relationships is to work with another teacher to observe a child who has been labeled a troublemaker. For two weeks each of you will aim to find something positive which this student accomplishes. During this time, you can support each other in the attempt to see beyond the negative behavior to a child who does not like what he is doing and needs your help to change. Keep brief notes and share them with each other. You will find that each of you is becoming more involved with the other and more skilled in seeing the strengths and unspoken needs of not only this child but also others.

We should know that looking for a person's strengths is a directive straight from the Torah. The Torah states that every child has "his way" – a nature of his own.[16] "…each of us has individual gifts and tendencies … A teacher should therefore not try to push all his students in a single direction. Instead, he should appreciate the gifts of each individual and cultivate their expression. Even when teaching the universal truths of the Torah, a teacher's goal should not be conformity. Instead, he should

---

16   Proverbs 22:6.

try to enable every student to internalize these truths in a manner that suits his own nature ... the development of true unity comes from a synthesis of different thrusts, every person expressing his own unique talents and personality."[17]

And from *Likutei Torah of the Arizal*, we learn that it is not proper to disdain the wealth *Hashem* bestows upon a person, be it material wealth or the person's talents. If this person "...had no need for it, *Hashem* would not have given it ... anything bestowed from above must be sought after."[18]

Let me assume that by now you can see how vital it is to reach toward the inner self of a student. Immediately you wonder how to accomplish this goal during the tightly-scheduled school day previously mentioned. Time, indeed, is scarce, but I discovered that many educators who are interested in creating ties with their students have actually been able to change this negative feature of a school day into a positive. The lack of ample time has forced these teachers to devise ingenious ways of finding out more about their students on a regular basis. One of these ways is to introduce a topic in the curriculum so that the subject-matter itself will produce details about students' lives. Carol Ann Tomlinson, professor of educational leadership, foundations, and policy at the University of Virginia, presents a scenario which shows us how to make use of subject-matter in this fashion. A science teacher, Mr. Johnson, and his fifth graders

---

17 Touger, 1995, 44-46.
18 *Likutei Torah of the Arizal, Vayishlach*, 96.

will be studying the topic of buoyancy. Mr. Johnson wants to make a link between science and his students' lives, so, at the beginning of the unit, he asks his students to think of times when some event, circumstance, or change in their lives made them "sink" or "float." He gives examples from his own life to make sure the students understand the activity. He allows his students to select the medium they want to use, e.g., a drawing with an explanation, or a written story, or a speech. His plan is to invite some students to be ready to share their examples, and he will encourage others to do the same. He doesn't stop here. He plans to guide his students in a discussion which will lead to principles that could explain why some humans "sink" and others "float."[19]

It is exciting to imagine how much will be revealed to Mr. Johnson when he reads or listens to the student responses. Even the choice of medium to use is an important piece of information for Mr. Johnson. Notice that in this scenario, the teacher will not be the only one who gains valuable insights. His students also will learn more about each other and about their teacher through the class discussions which will follow. I see two goals that have been accomplished: everyone in this classroom has been enabled to look beyond the surface of each other, and the students have become more invested in the topic of buoyancy. Mr. Johnson's introduction to a science topic has built connective tissue.

While exploring the disservice that comes from

---

19 Tomlinson, 2003, 69, 71.

labeling children, I became acquainted with a related problem – the complex nature of making a diagnosis. In the previously mentioned book, *Cries Unheard*, George Halasz and his colleagues challenge us to rethink the interpretation of children's problem behavior as necessarily a marker of illness. As we saw earlier, these writers are especially concerned about the growing medicalization of children's problem behavior, especially in the case of ADHD.

Anne Manne writes, "While many doctors accept the existence of some kind of ADHD type condition which may respond to drugs like Ritalin, a wide range of specialists have expressed their concern over the sudden increase in apparent sufferers, the long term consequences of drug use, the possibility of a manufactured epidemic, the grey area of possible misdiagnosis, the confusion over causation, and the nebulous nature of the symptoms. One of the world's most eminent child psychiatrists, Sir Michael Rutter, has said that for a diagnosis to be useful it must be distinctive from other disorders in its causation, natural progression and treatment. His view is that ADHD, as currently defined, does not satisfy these requirements."[20]

Based on this opinion, another researcher concludes that the unproven status of ADHD "should give pause to both researchers and clinicians who may have reified ADHD as a 'thing' or 'true entity' (rather than a working hypothesis...)."[21]

---

20 Diller, 1999, p. 63, quoted in Halasz et al, 2002, 9.
21 Halasz et al, 2002, 77.

It seems, then, that ADHD does refer to a set of symptoms, but we are not sure that it is a diagnosis. Halasz has explored what could be behind these symptoms and presents the idea that these symptoms may represent a reaction to an attachment deficit at some point in the child's life. If this deficit has indeed occurred, he argues that now the parent(s) and child can be helped to establish a healthy relationship, and to the extent that their insecure attachment patterns are repaired, the original symptoms should fade away.[22]

Halasz and his colleagues are especially concerned that gaining understanding about the conditions underlying the above-described symptoms is being sabotaged by the policies of insurance companies, the reduction in spending in general to pay for mental health personnel, and the pressure to find a quick solution to classroom management difficulties. These practices lead to the prescribing of drugs as the first choice of treatment rather than one of the last. Halasz acknowledges that medication can be useful, but it is overprescribed and too often not connected to needed therapy. Ellingsen expresses concisely the objection to the irrational numbing down of people:

---

22 See also "Suffer the Restless Children – Unsettling Questions about the ADHD Label" in *What to Look For in a Classroom ... and Other Essays* by Alfie Kohn, 1998. This chapter presents observations that are strikingly similar to those of Halasz. Kohn cites studies by American researchers showing that distractibility and/or hyperactivity were significantly correlated with maternal anxiety/aggression and intrusive caregiving as well as other family variables like the level of emotional support given to young children.

"Our emotional responses are not viruses to be suppressed, but meanings to be unpacked."[23]

Five years after *Cries Unheard* was published, a tragedy occurred which substantiates the viewpoints of Halasz and his colleagues. A four-year-old girl died in Hull, Massachusetts, and the parents were charged with deliberately giving their daughter overdoses of prescription drugs to sedate her. According to police reports, the girl had been taking a potent cocktail of psychiatric drugs since age two, when she was given a diagnosis of attention deficit disorder and bipolar disorder. The particular cause of her death, if proven, is a tragedy in itself, but this case and the ensuing debate which it sparked among psychiatrists point to the possibility that a broader tragedy is occurring.[24] Several psychiatrists are quoted in this article,[25] and their comments are a striking confirmation of the concerns raised in *Cries Unheard*.

Here is a sampling of the comments: "Bipolar is absolutely being overdiagnosed in children, and the major downside is that people then think they have a solution and are not amenable to listening to alternatives... Parents very often want a quick fix, and doctors rarely have much time to spend with them, and the great appeal of prescribing a medication is that it's simple..."[26]

---

23 Halasz et al, 2002, 58.
24 *New York Times*, Feb. 15, 2007, A17.
25 Ibid.
26 Dr. Gabrielle Carlson, professor of psychiatry and pediatrics at Stony Brook University School of Medicine, Long Island.

"Most of the patients I see who have been misdiagnosed have been told they have bipolar disorder... The diagnosis is made with no understanding of the context of their life. Then they're put on these devastating medications and condemned to a life as a psychiatry patient."[27]

Teachers, psychiatrists, and early childhood specialists aren't the only ones who may suffer from "premature closure," a term used by Dr. Mark Graber, chief of medical service at the VA Medical Center in Northport, N.Y. Dr. Graber defines premature closure as "the tendency to focus on one diagnosis that seems to explain all of the symptoms, then stop considering other possibilities."[28] His comments are part of an article[29] on preventing medical misdiagnosis. One tool developed to help doctors is an online diagnostic aid called the Isabel system, which processes symptoms and presents possible diagnoses. Its use is part of a culture change for doctors, who are having to face the fact that they can't really know it all or carry in their heads all the medical knowledge they need. Other programs include prompts to get doctors and nurses to ask patients and/or families a series of carefully prepared questions. Specific aids like these could help parents, teachers, and education specialists to maintain the viewpoint that children are always evolving and that diagnoses are most often only working hypotheses.

27 Dr. Bessel van der Kolk, professor of psychiatry at Boston University.
28 *Wall Street Journal*, Nov. 29, 2006, D5.
29 Ibid.

Note the statement by Dr. Bessel van der Kolk[30] that many doctors make diagnoses with no understanding of the context of their patients' lives. This practice needs to be avoided in the field of education as well. Educators need more knowledge about the context of their students' lives. One possible solution is for a school to develop a brief family history form that allows parents to relate occurrences in their lives and their own parents' lives that may increase a teacher's understanding of their child. These comments would remain confidential and could be kept in the child's file. At designated times during the year, teachers could ask their parents if they have anything to add to their child's family history. An ongoing file like this could help in two ways: it could provide progressive information to those working with a student, and it could create a channel for teachers and parents to collaborate.

I hope that this chapter has encouraged you to recall your own memories and stories and that, together with mine, they will fuel an unquenchable desire to create classrooms where the promotion of personhood happens on a regular basis. Trying out a suggestion or two in this chapter may be the beginning of our endeavors to find out as much as we can about who our students really are and not to succumb to tenuous conclusions rendered by a label.

We must be careful, however, to place the idea of personhood within a Torah context, lest

---

30   See note 25.

it degenerate into a narrow focus on the self that leaves little room for others. It is all too easy to see that we live at a time when self-fulfillment as a worthwhile goal is widely accepted, but pursuing this goal can become unbalanced and lead, more often than not, to an unhealthy emphasis on the ego. To keep a proper balance, we must ask ourselves, "Why do we need to find out as much as we can about who our students really are?" And a second question, "Why does a student need to know as much as he can about himself?"

To answer these questions, the staff and students in Jewish schools possess a tremendous advantage. They have access to the Torah's explanation of why *Hashem* gives each person particular talents and tendencies in a combination that is not duplicated in any other person. The Torah tells us that each student who enters our schools has a unique purpose for being, and this purpose is directly related to the reason for the existence of the entire universe. *Hashem* creates this physical world in order to have a home here, where His presence is most concealed. This is *Hashem's* desire.[31] He is "waiting," so to speak, for a Jew to come along and do something that will keep his little corner of the world moving forward on the course set by *Hashem*. When a Jew does something that is aligned with the will of *Hashem*, he reveals *Hashem's* presence in the very order of existence that most denies it. As mentioned above, every individual is equipped with particular talents and tendencies; these are his

---

31   *Tanchuma, Naso* 16.

resources, and they can now be seen as precisely the tools he needs to uncover the G-dliness hidden in the area of his influence. *Hashem* has an assignment for each of us that cannot be performed by anyone else. It stands to reason that the more a teacher knows his student, the more he will be able to help him find out why he is needed in this world. For this endeavor, labels are of little use.

2
Avoiding A March Through The Curriculum With A Prescribed One-Size-Fits-All Method

To create a well-functioning classroom, we need to remove unproductive barriers between teacher and students and between students and subject matter. Our problem is that these barriers to communication and engagement are built into classrooms preoccupied with covering a prescribed curriculum within a specified time. Typically a teacher is given a curriculum which he is to follow so that his students will be prepared for the next grade. The need to be "prepared" for the next grade and for the upcoming standardized tests becomes the driving force of instruction and puts intense pressure on a teacher to keep moving through material rather than to teach for understanding. The outcome of this hurried movement through material is a superficial, often rote type of learning which serves no one well. In addition, this classroom will most certainly contain students who vary in needs and capabilities; in other words, the "one-size-fits-all" has never fit all, so schools often adopt the policy of dividing a class into supposed "ability" groups or placing children in ability tracks. This arrangement is problematic in many ways, beginning with the decision-making process for dividing the class, the selection of materials and goals for each group, and the typical lack of connectedness between one group and another. Such a policy begs the question: if only some of our students have access to quality materials and experiences that demand an appropriate level of higher-order thinking, how can we say that tracking is a good educational practice? The decision to make ability groups appears to be initiated most often by pressure from interested parties rather than by a careful consideration of educational alternatives. In the general studies division, what can easily happen is that children at each level are given work that appears on graphically beautiful pages produced by a textbook company. Even at the highest level, the activities, although they may be more interesting, often lack a sense of purpose and ignore foundational skills that are necessary to do them with a sense of real understanding. In informal conversations with children in the highest levels and with their parents, I have discovered that a child often will need his parents' help to uncover the thought process required to answer a given item. Many times the teacher may not be aware that the child cannot do a number of the activities independently.

My overriding concern with this arrangement, however, is the effect that it has on busy teachers and

Avoiding A March Through The Curriculum With A Prescribed One-Size-Fits-All Method

their children as, day by day, they view each other as objects that have been sorted, much as maple syrup, for example, is given different grades. Even if the less advanced children make some progress, at least two questions remain: How is progress being defined for them? And how can the teacher decide that the progress of these students reflects their true potential? He has no way to compare the tracked arrangement with other solutions, and other solutions do exist. Teachers need to consider the evidence that less able children, in a prepared and stimulating environment, learn much from their more advanced peers. When the opportunity for this kind of learning is not available because tracking has been chosen as the solution, all the students literally soak up inaccurate messages. The higher level students feel a certain success; they are the "good" ones, as one student said, inadvertently. I am not sure that these students' sense of success has much clarity to it; it is probably being narrowly defined, in an unexamined way, as being able to answer questions the teacher gives them. For the middle and lowest groups, students may feel a kind of relief that they are not facing constant frustration, but I feel certain that they know, subconsciously and sometimes consciously, that they have been undervalued, that in some way they are less worthwhile. They have lost out on the affirmation component so vital to being able to learn well.

    To support the above argument in concrete ways, I have drawn once again on the work of Carol Ann Tomlinson. She gives the example of Lydia, who appears to have a learning disability. "Everyone is working hard with Lydia to help her compensate for her learning problems."[1] The teacher is making adjustments, the learning disabilities specialist works with her, and her mom helps with homework. Tomlinson writes her version of this student's experience: "Lydia works hard, but the work seems so rote. It's the same thing year after year. Her mind thinks about important things, but no one ever asks her to write or think about important things… The other students, by contrast, seem to spend more time on ideas and less on spelling and commas and handwriting. Maybe that means she is not really capable of doing important things. Lydia lacks a sense of purpose and cognitive challenge in her work. It makes her think her disability defines her rather than her abilities."[2]

Here is another example. In several subjects Beth is at least three or four years ahead of grade expectations in knowledge and skill. Her teacher praises her generously and wants to affirm Beth's ability "and to give her a sense of the power she has …"[3] Again, Tomlinson describes Beth's experience with this class: "Beth has a sense that she is not important in the classroom. If she were, the teacher would know she is only repeating things she has long since learned rather than challenging herself. The work … does not seem purposeful to her and does not absorb her. And she somehow feels dishonest because the teacher tells her she is doing excellent work when she knows she makes high

---

1 Tomlinson, 2003, 24.
2 Ibid.
3 Ibid., 23.

grades with no effort...."[4]

Nancie Atwell gives us yet another example. In her book, *Side by Side*, she describes her experience with a learning-disabled student who moved from a resource room and special class of low-tracked students to her "regular" eighth grade English class. In this class, which had become a writing and reading workshop, Laura overcame her classification as a special education student and became "an accomplished writer and reader."[5] In her new workshop situation, she found herself in a classroom of twenty-five teachers. "Everyone learns from everybody, and less able students may learn most and best of all. Surrounded by more able models, learners whose ideas will spark and charge the environment, special education students have equal access to complex and worthwhile activities."[6] Atwell tells us that during a four-year period of including learning-disabled students in her classroom, all of them succeeded, and no one returned to the resource room.

Atwell gives us examples of Laura's writing – excerpts from her reading journal, a letter she wrote to an author, Judy Blume, an interview of Nancie Atwell, and an amazing free-verse poem, her first, titled "All We Know." This poem grew from Laura's feelings about Christa McAuliffe, a social studies teacher who lost her life, together with six others, when the Challenger space shuttle exploded. Finally, we have the privilege of reading

4   Ibid.
5   Atwell, 1991, 19.
6   Ibid., 21.

a letter Laura wrote to Mikhail Gorbachev urging him to seek a peaceful international policy. She wanted to use an epigraph at the beginning of her letter, and after searching through a collection of poems by Robert Frost, she chose "A Time to Talk." The combination of this poem and her letter is stunning, and she won second prize for it in a contest sponsored by Rotary Club International.

At this point it is useful to look at the practice of including resource rooms as part of a school's services. The purpose of a resource room is to provide a teacher who can help students who have been diagnosed with learning disabilities or who have other issues. Schools may have a resource room for general studies and one for Torah and Hebrew language studies. When resource rooms have been functioning within a school for a few years, the number of students needing them seems to increase.

I would like you to consider the possibility that the resource room and the increased demand for it will inevitably accompany a classroom that is built around the idea that every student will rely on the same textbook, proceed through it at the same pace, with more or less the same methods, and will "finish" this material by the end of the year. Under these conditions, most, if not all, of the students in any class will not be able to fit their learning into this design. I have already described the most common response to this problem, the formation of homogeneous ability groups, with generous use of the resource room when spaces are available.

Given the above powerful examples of Tomlinson

and Atwell, could it be that if classrooms were set up in ways that allow each child to learn, the need for a resource room would all but fade away, except, perhaps, for truly unusual students? The positive aspects of the resource room – the small size of the group and the focus on the specific needs of each child – can be incorporated into the way the regular classroom functions.[7]

All of us have heard that there are two ways to look at a partially filled cup of water; it can be described as half empty or half full. The half full description can be a way of looking at our present situation in education. In every teacher's past, there is much good. On the other hand, there is still a greater good to come. To reach out for this greater good requires that we look at our classrooms with new eyes, that we attempt a paradigm shift. We need to loosen up our thoughts, let go of our already-forming objections, and follow our deepest aspirations, much as we would advise one of our own students to do.

I deeply aspire for classrooms whose teachers routinely search for respectful ways to reach all students, ways which will not diminish any individual's dignity or falsely inflate his

---

[7] See the topic, "Use Small Group Instruction as a Regular Part of Instructional Cycles," Tomlinson, 2003, 84.

The special education teacher can then be used as a consultant who shares her expertise with classroom teachers. She will be able to fine-tune her recommendations because of her increased exposure to classrooms that are demanding and, at the same time, supportive of everyone's success. See also "Team with Resource Specialists," 87.

accomplishments. To nourish this aspiration, all of us can try to recall scenes from our own teaching experiences where we knew, beyond any doubt, that something real was taking place.

Here are two examples: A teacher of four-year-olds presents to her children the idea of words that rhyme. She reads a charming, simple story with rhyming words at the end of each line. She reads it several times and then begins to pause before the end of each line, and the children, like a chorus, gleefully supply the missing words. Another time the teacher starts a rhyming chant, with a strong beat, and the children supply the missing word in each verse. (This time they haven't heard the chant beforehand.) One day out on the playground, several students come running across the entire length of the school yard to tell her some rhyming pairs that they discovered while talking together. The scene changes. This teacher asks a four-year-old what he would say to *Hashem* if he could stand at the Western Wall, the Kotel, in Jerusalem. The child responds with the following: "*Hashem*, why don't You speak to us like You did in the olden days? You can do it, *Hashem*. You have the power!"

These children were learning and communicating with their teacher not because they wanted a sticker or a good grade or even a pat on the back. Their learning was like breathing – it simply is what is done. Look back at some of the classes you have taught for moments like these, when you could sense that the whole child was responding to you, giving you a window into his inner life. Savor the pleasure of such moments and imagine that you are a teacher in a classroom that has come to be characterized by such encounters.

To imagine such a classroom, at any age-level and on any subject, we need to have a model of best education practices and then assistance in implementing them. I found certain educators to be immensely helpful as I was trying to understand what a trackless classroom of mixed-ability and highly engaged learners would look like. I have already referred to Donna Goertz, Carol Ann Tomlinson, Nancie Atwell, Angeline Lillard, Parker Palmer, Daniel Goleman, Vivian Gussin Paley, and Alfie Kohn. I also learned from Maria Montessori, Howard Gardner, Thomas Armstrong, and Jay McTighe. To my great satisfaction, I found in the life and writings of many of our great Torah leaders the deep foundation for the concepts presented by these contemporary educators. They all share amazingly similar interests and values. Although their styles, the wider context within which they operate, and their depth of understanding may differ, they are bound together by an unwavering loyalty to the inestimable worth of a human being. They all stress the necessity of teachers and students becoming observers of their own behavior, of having time to reflect, of uncovering personal meaning in their work, of learning how to evaluate their own work, of being able to choose work, of constantly moving a bit beyond what is already known to reach ever higher levels of independence, of taking time to listen to the other, of learning and producing with others, of discovering strengths and developing them, and of learning how to look at conflict as an opportunity. I have no doubt that all of us would claim these necessities as our own, but they seem to slip through our fingers as we face the daily grind. Again, we need a model that will enable us to focus on these necessities and that will translate them into concrete practices.

I offer for your consideration one possible model, developed by Carol Ann Tomlinson in her book, *Fulfilling the Promise of the Differentiated Classroom*. I like her model because her descriptions of the necessary elements and their relationships to each other echo the voices of the educators I just mentioned. When a teacher plans with this model in mind, he is prompted to ask himself if the activities he is considering are the kind that students will find engaging, purposeful, and empowering.

Before we explore this model, we need an explanation of the term, "differentiated classroom." This classroom is similar to any classroom in that it contains students who differ in readiness, talents, and interests. The mark of a differentiated classroom is its attitude toward these differences. The fact that a classroom of students is not homogeneous is seen as normal and, even, desirous. The teacher presents the same meaningful, significant understandings to all the students but varies the related activities and tasks to make them suitable for each student. Since everyone has his "portion" in the knowledge, skills, and understandings which the teacher presents, he is able to make a contribution to his class. Such classrooms are characterized by much sharing and respect. The environment requires from the teacher continuous thought and meticulous planning.

Avoiding A March Through The Curriculum With A Prescribed One-Size-Fits-All Method

The room is arranged to promote small and large group meetings. It contains multi-level resources. Students share with their teacher responsibility for the success of the classroom. Although direct teaching occurs in a differentiated classroom, the active nature of the learning gives it the feel of a workshop. The curriculum becomes the medium through which the teacher and his students continue to learn about and respond to each other. Practical steps to achieve such a classroom will be included in the pages of this book.

Tomlinson chooses two metaphors to begin her description of responsive teaching. The first one is the story of taming a fox, taken from S. Exupery's book *The Little Prince*. In this book a young boy and a fox establish ties with each other; they begin to need each other and to see each other as unique "in all the world." In the end, they must part physically, but they are joined forever by the times they shared.

Tomlinson uses this metaphor to underscore the relationship between teacher (the young boy) and student (the fox) in a differentiated classroom. The teacher shows up each day with patience and with the intent to listen. He begins to understand what is essential about each learner. In this process (and in the story), both parties are teachers, and both are learners. Tomlinson acknowledges that there are things teachers are supposed to know – ideas, skills, and understandings, but a teacher in a differentiated classroom is willing to be a vulnerable learner, to take risks each day as his own understandings are clarified by the mystery of each of the lives in his classroom.

The Hebrew language itself points to the nature of teacher as learner. Rabbi Moshe M. Eisemann explains that the Hebrew word, "to teach," is derived from the Hebrew word, "to learn." They share the same root – the Hebrew letters *lamed, mem, dalet*.[8] "In the Torah's view, the act of teaching, to be true to its ideal nature, must be an intensified act of learning."[9]

Rabbi Eisemann recalls for us the kind of teacher who believes that he has "everything down pat" and is not interested in being challenged by a student's fresh approach or new perspective. Such a teacher has lost the opportunity to use his student's challenge "to polish and sharpen his own understanding..."[10] The greater harm, though, is that in rejecting the challenge, he is also rejecting his student.

Tomlinson continues, "...we teach responsively when we understand the need to teach the human beings before us as well as to teach the content with which we are charged. In a time when teachers feel almost unbearable pressure to standardize what we do, it is important to begin with the conviction that we are no longer teaching if what we teach is more important than who we teach or how we teach."[11]

Tomlinson's second metaphor is a set of three cogs that depicts key elements in the differentiated classroom. The three cogs are similar to three

---

8   Eisemann, 28.
9   Ibid., 29.
10   Ibid.
11   Tomlinson, 2003, 10.

gears, interrelated and interdependent. The first cog represents the needs of the student. The second represents the role of the teacher. The third represents the role of curriculum and instruction. In the first cog are what the student seeks: affirmation, contribution, power, purpose, and challenge. The second cog lays out the teacher's response to these needs in the form of invitation, opportunity, investment, persistence, and reflection. The third cog presents curriculum and instruction as the teacher's medium for attending to what the learner seeks. Curriculum, therefore, must be important, focused, engaging, demanding, and scaffolded.[12]

Tomlinson assures us that all of the above elements in each of these three cogs "...are rooted in our current understanding of the psychology of teaching and learning, our escalating knowledge of the brain, and our long experience in observing and learning from daily interactions in countless classrooms."[13]

These two metaphors (taming the fox and the connected cogs) provide a useful model for understanding differentiation. Tomlinson carefully fills out the meaning of each of the fifteen elements mentioned above and then shows us how to translate these elements into concrete practices. As we proceed along with her, we begin to acquire the language necessary to explain why certain teachers in our own lives will always be a source of strength.

---

12 "Scaffolded" is a term borrowed from the building industry and is used in the sense of providing the support required to enable a student to "work" at a higher level.

13 Tomlinson, 12.

(We are joined forever by the times we shared.) We also begin to be able to discern what was missing in many of our other encounters. In other words, we now have a vantage point from which we can assess our present goals and practices. To get a real grasp of how well student needs, teacher responses, and curriculum and instruction can and do work together requires a careful reading of Tomlinson's book. For our purposes, it is helpful to consider her memories of an eighth grade algebra teacher and a German language teacher she had a year later. Both teachers "...were solid with curriculum. They both instructed with confidence. The difference was that the first teacher taught algebra. The second teacher taught me German.... 'Please invest in me,' I said to both teachers. One teacher responded, 'The information is here. I'll deliver it. You get it.' The other said, 'I will learn about you and do whatever it takes, using this subject matter, to make sure you are a fuller and more potent human being than you were when you walked in this room. Please be my colleague in that quest.'"[14] With curriculum and instruction as the medium, this latter teacher was able to show her student "...the power of knowledge, the power of self, and the inextricable links between the two."[15]

I have selected one element from each of the three cogs and will show how Tomlinson defines each.

---

14 Ibid., 57, 58.
15 Ibid.

Power (a student need) is characterized by the following statements:
- ~ What I learn is useful to me now.
- ~ I make choices that contribute to my success.
- ~ I understand how this place operates and what is expected of me.
- ~ I know what quality looks like here and how to achieve it.
- ~ There is dependable support here for my journey.[16]

Investment (a teacher response) implies the following:
- ~ I work hard to make this place work for you.
- ~ I work to make this place reflect you.
- ~ I enjoy thinking about what we do here.
- ~ I love to find new paths to success.
- ~ It is my job to help you succeed.
- ~ I am your partner in growth.
- ~ I will do what it takes to ensure your growth.[17]

Engaging (a description of curriculum and instruction) means the following:
- ~ Students most often find meaning in their work.
- ~ Students most often find the work intriguing.

---

16 Ibid., 16.
17 Ibid., 28.

~ Students see themselves and their world in the work.
~ Students see value to others in the work.
~ Students find the work provokes their curiosity.
~ Students often find themselves absorbed by the work.[18]

Paradigm shift, indeed. But teachers are doing it. If we decide to join them, we have not only their example but also a sizeable network of interested and talented educators. This network is easily accessed through books, articles, audiotapes, videos, websites, and on-line courses. The Association for Supervision and Curriculum Development in Virginia is an excellent place to start. The final page of Tomlinson's book lists numerous resources from this organization.

One of these resources is a video entitled "A Visit to a Differentiated Classroom." This 60-minute video is an exciting way to see how one teacher and her students (third- and fourth-graders together!) operate in a differentiated classroom in a public school. Among the many things you will view are the following: the children entering their room and finding instructions ready for them, the arrangement of the furniture to accommodate whole-class and small-group meetings, and the teacher moving about from one group to another, checking, probing, and explaining. You will see her showing a small group of students different kinds

---

18   Ibid., 59.

Avoiding A March Through The Curriculum With A Prescribed One-Size-Fits-All Method

of questions they will encounter on standardized tests ("inside the text" types and "beyond the text" types). You will see her eliciting information sources from her students, with instructions to share this information with others; you will see students cleaning and straightening their classroom and doing other functions which were done, in the past, by the teacher. And you will see an amazing rubric on the wall and will be able to watch students actually using it to evaluate their work for that day.

Another stimulating resource is a book entitled *Integrating Differentiated Instruction and Understanding by Design* by Carol Ann Tomlinson and Jay McTighe, published in 2006. I appreciate the courage of both these authors in addressing questions like the following: How does the teacher use content and performance standards without falling into the pit of standardization? How does a teacher grade students in a differentiated classroom? How does a teacher begin the process of using new teaching practices that push her beyond her comfort level? These questions, together with useful guidelines and concrete examples, will be explored in the fourth chapter of this book. For now, I refer you to a section of *Fulfilling the Promise* entitled "Toolbox." In its sixty-three pages, Tomlinson has reprinted actual student surveys, an amazing schedule chart, checklists of student skills, rubrics, a planning guide for students, a peer critique guide, an evaluation checklist, and many more such items.

One simple rubric[19] especially caught my eye as a powerful example of how helpful such a tool can be to students. Imagine a grid with five squares across and four squares down. The grid is divided into four levels, listed in the vertical column to the far left:

    1. **Getting Started** (Novice), represented by a seed underground.
    2. **Almost** (Apprentice), represented by the seed forming roots and pushing up slightly.
    3. **Got It!** (Practitioner), represented by a sprout with a bud and leaves.
    4. **Wow!** (Expert), represented by a completely opened flower and its leaves.

The next vertical column from the left is Science Tools; the next is Science Concepts; the next is Reasoning Strategies, and the last, on the far right, is Communication. A student reads the entire rubric before he starts to work, and he can recheck himself as he goes along to see what needs to be accomplished in order to get to a higher quality level.

I was also intrigued by the daily schedule chart.[20] It is divided into a grid and has a symbol in each square representing the type of work to be done by the students. The students' names are on clothespins so that they can be easily moved to change group composition or size. What is so

---

19   Ibid., 112.
20   Ibid., 106.

appealing is that the students themselves see the organization of their day and learn how to follow it on their own. In this particular chart, there are no more than four children in each group, and the chart contains several "student choice" squares, represented by a large question mark.

As noted earlier, Tomlinson sees the developing bond between teacher and student as the foundation for responsive teaching. Similarly, great Torah educators tell us that when a student is learning from a teacher whom he trusts, he is able to internalize the messages of the Torah. Rabbi Klein writes, "The bond between teacher and student, if established along the lines of Torah, is unparalleled by any other bond between any two parties. The Maharal's view is that nothing can be as intense."[21] And in Reb Simcha Wasserman's words, "Torah is given *b'ahavah* – with love – and it creates a close relationship between student and teacher. A general principle in teaching Torah subjects is that the students should be thought of as the teacher's children. Only Torah creates this kind of relationship, and it does so in a natural way."[22]

Although the learning of Torah is distinct from any other learning, the dynamic of bonding appears to be an essential piece in both secular and Judaic studies. Ideally, there should be a seamless flow between the two, since secular studies describe the details of *Hashem's* creation and can consciously be presented in this way. For practical reasons,

---

21 Klein, 2001, 92.
22 Branfman and Tatz, 1994, 78.

we separate general studies and Judaic studies, but a person doesn't live two lives – one, a general studies life, and the other, a Judaic studies life. Quality (in character development and academic learning) in one area will spill over into quality in the other; likewise, lack of quality in one area will find its way to the other. Internalizing Torah values keeps us from falling for the notion that one can compartmentalize one's life and still remain Torah-true. To be morally healthy and even more – to be holy, a Jew is directed to know G-d in all his ways.[23] Ideally, then, school should become a natural place for a student to work on his character during every part of his day.

The relational aspect of education takes on even more significance when seen in the light of recent research in infant and child development, including the *Hardwired to Connect* report. This research is supporting the hypothesis that a healthy bonding between mother (or primary caregiver) and infant leads to a positive development of the infant's brain and the infant's behaviors as he grows in his early years. On the other hand, if this bonding or attachment process is characterized by anxiety, ambivalence, inconsistency, or unavailability on the part of the mother, the infant is at great risk for becoming depressed and for later exhibiting symptoms such as over-activity, inability to concentrate, and distractibility. If the family, including the infant, enters an intensive therapy program designed to repair the break in the

---

23   Proverbs 3:6.

Avoiding A March Through The Curriculum With A Prescribed One-Size-Fits-All Method

attachment process, both the infant and the parents can make an amazing about-face, in a relatively short period of time. "A number of young children aged between three and five years have been referred to clinicians with a query as to whether they have ADHD. It is striking how quickly their frenetic behaviour lessens *once they feel they are being communicated with and taken seriously.*"[24] (emphasis mine)

Researchers also have found that in many cases, children's negative behavior patterns seem to be linked to early care that is less individualized and less sensitively adapted to the child's needs.

If educators will take a moment to reflect on the above discoveries about child development,[25] I feel they will come away with another argument in favor of the differentiated classroom as described by Tomlinson. As she states so often in her book, a child who is learning is a child who is being taken seriously and whose needs are being met.

Note also the amazing parallel between an infant's quick recovery, with the proper intervention, and the young man's recovery at Gateshead, previously described. Here is yet another example, taken from a letter to the editor in *Hamodia*.[26] A mother writes that her son, "basically a very gentle and good boy," wasted five years of his life at an out-of-town *mesivta*. She and her husband were unaware of how poorly he was doing until they were notified that, unless he improved, he would be thrown out. Their

---

24 Halasz et al, 2002, 71.
25 Reported in Halasz's book and in *Hardwired to Connect*.
26 April 7, 2000, 54.

son had never complained, and they "were in awe of the *Rosh Yeshiva*, who never had a good word to say about our son." The boy braved it out until time to switch to a *yeshiva gedola*. Through a suggestion of one of his teachers, the parents enrolled him in a small yeshiva with a warm and caring rosh yeshiva. With the *Rosh Yeshiva's* constant encouragement, this student became a different person. The journey was not easy, but the parents began to get "beautiful reports" as the rabbinical staff lifted his self-esteem and showed they believed in him. The mother ends her letter with this plea: "I beg all *rebbeim* and *maggidei shiur* to please be aware that a *gut vort* can take a student much further than constant reprimands and censure. Does not *Shlomo Hamelech* advise us to teach each child according to his ways?"

The above child development research, coupled with Tomlinson's work, led me to apply the importance of healthy bonding to our relationship with *Hashem*. After all, one of several ways that we relate to *Hashem* is that of a child to his father. There is a bond here, also. On the deepest level, this bond with *Hashem* cannot be severed. We must still, however, answer what is going to be our attitude toward this bond. Will we embrace it, try to run away from it, ignore it, or not even know that it exists? The formation of this attitude, whether positive or negative, begins at home. It will be built from particular experiences, ranging all the way from rich ones to nearly none, depending on the parents. Soon the child begins to spend most of his day at a Jewish school. Now his *morahs* and *rebbeim* will play a large part in how he views his relationship with *Hashem*. Seen in this light, I would imagine that every Judaics teacher would be strongly motivated to learn how to respond to every student's need for affirmation, contribution, power, purpose, and challenge. (Tomlinson's concepts) Again, recall Tomlinson's elements of teacher response: invitation, opportunity, investment, persistence, and reflection. If these student needs and teacher responses apply to the general studies curriculum, all the more so do they apply to the study of Torah. In our Judaics classrooms we must learn how to make our every act, the expression on our faces, and the tone of our voices reflect our deep respect for each student and our belief in him as a vital player in *Hashem's* grand design for the universe. If our young people, expert as they are in reading hidden messages, sense that their teachers are genuinely invested in them, they will emerge from these classrooms with a growing sense of confidence in *Hashem's* constant watchfulness and support of their lives.

Having a taste of both Tomlinson's model and the idea of the bond between *Hashem* and each Jew, we can confront the appearance of an unmotivated student in a Gemara class. This middle-school student cannot or will not relate to Gemara. The traditional method of learning Gemara is simply not working for him. He is already in a self-defeating spiral caused by previous negative experiences, and the school staff has so far not offered him or his parents any alternatives to this dead-end situation. After any discussion, the parents are always left with the conclusion that their son is at fault.

I see two questions begging to be answered in this scenario. Firstly, what is more important, Gemara or this young Jew? Moshe Rabbeinu has already answered this question in parshas Ki Sisa, 32:32. Faced with the possibility that *Hashem* might destroy the Jewish people because of the sin of the Golden Calf, Moshe responded, "If You would, forgive their sin. And if not, please obliterate me from the book You have written." The depth of Moshe's bond with the Jewish people forms the conclusion of the entire Torah. The closing verse refers to Moshe's breaking of the first tablets. As explained in *The Garden of the Torah*, "...when the future of the Jewish people was at stake, Moshe was willing to break the tablets without hesitation. Why did Moshe take such a step? Because there is nothing – not even the Torah – which G-d cherishes more than a Jew."[27] Secondly, just how much is a rebbe supposed to care about his student? Again, we already know what the Torah answers – as much as he can, and then more so. He must develop a love for his student even if he perceives his student at first to be like a stranger.[28]

On the concept of a single student as a whole

---

27 Touger, 1995, 158.

28 See *The Art of Education* by Rabbi Yitzchak Ginsburgh for an in-depth discussion of the bonding that must occur between a student and his teacher. In this book the reader will discover, within the framework of Kabbala and Chassidus, every major concept which I found in the secular literature on education.

universe, consider the following, from Rabbi Ginsburgh's book, *The Art of Education*: "Every child, every student, is as complex, deep and intriguing as any tractate of the Talmud that scholars pour over for days and years."[29] Add to this perception the following expression by Rabbi Isaac Hutner. He said, "Rabbi [so-and-so, a brilliant Talmudic lecturer,] stays awake until two in the morning analyzing a *Tosafos*. I stay awake until two in the morning analyzing a student."[30]

Finally, we can draw on the advice of the Lubavitcher Rebbe, Rabbi Menachem Mendel Schneerson. He instructed that you (a teacher) must approach each Jew (your student) as though you were an emissary sent by the King of kings to talk with the prince, the King's only son. The Rebbe also writes, "Even when children are obedient, or when one's influence is so strong that a simple word to the students is sufficient, one must not think that he has done enough. Even in such cases one must exert oneself in their education."[31] All the more so must one exert oneself with students who appear to be drifting away.

From all these words of Torah, the unmistakable conclusion is that our Gemara rebbe must develop his will to find other ways to reach this student. He could start with his own soul-searching and reflection. He could bounce ideas around with his

---

29   Ginsburgh, 2005, 14.
30   Reported by Rabbi Simcha Krauss, interview of July 1988, in *Illuminating the Generations* by Rabbi Hillel Goldberg, 1992, 118.
31   Schneerson, 1983, 6.

colleagues. He could look for *rebbeim* and other educators who have worked specifically with students like these. One such educator is Rabbi Yakov Horowitz, who shares his experiences with at-risk Jewish adolescents in a book titled *Living and Parenting: A Down-to-Earth Guide*. Rabbi Horowitz writes of the despair that he kept seeing in the eyes and hearts of underachieving teens in Jewish schools. In a succession of fifty short but powerful chapters, he offers clear and practical advice to teachers and parents on how to reverse the spiral of defeat and estrangement felt by a growing number of our youth. I noticed the importance he attaches to being able to instruct in more than one modality, especially when young students are trying to follow the logic of a complex passage in Gemara. He also urges *rebbeim* not to rely on "picking it up as you go" when their students are learning a language. Students will benefit from being taught, in an explicit manner, the basic skills they need in order to read Hebrew and Aramaic.

While our Gemara rebbe is looking around for advice, it may occur to him that middle-school-aged boys need a Torah class about the big questions in every Jew's life, e.g., Why am I here? What does *Hashem* really want from me? If the Torah is timeless and contains all the answers, why doesn't it speak to me? Does anyone else feel the same way I do? Obviously, the students in such a class must feel free and safe to ask what is really on their minds. The rebbe for this class may need some assistance in opening himself up and helping others to open up. He can fortify himself by remembering that the Torah is the one source that can deal with any question, and he should learn to demonstrate to his students his own humility (and, possibly, pain) in the face of a question which doesn't have an easy answer or which may require him to do some homework of his own. Whether in general studies or Torah studies, a teacher benefits from viewing his students' questions as avenues to greater understanding. The more difficult, penetrating, even off-the-wall such questions may be, the more complete will be the resulting grasp of a subject for both the student and his teacher. I do not advocate setting up this kind of class only for those who cannot learn Gemara. That would be falling back into old, unproductive habits, especially when we know that every Jew has questions like these at some time in his life.

While pondering this problem, I thought of another suggestion. Offer to this student some well-written and suspense-filled stories that have a Torah context. Find out which ones he enjoyed and converse with him about the story in the same fashion that you would with your own colleagues. Ask your student if he has ever had to confront a situation like the one in the story. Does he like the main character? Whom does he dislike, and why? Has he ever been in a dangerous neighborhood? Has he ever had a hard choice to make? If he tells the truth in a given situation, what does he think will be the consequences for him? Whom does he trust? Did any of the characters in the story have a problem with trust?

If you sense that a particular story really engaged

him, ask him if he would like to turn it into a play and invite his peers to be the actors, prop-costume suppliers, and any other roles needed to produce this play and perform it for the fifth graders in his school. If this idea appeals to him, tell him that you will give him the support needed to accomplish this project.

You may ask, "What does this have to do with Gemara?" It has everything to do with Gemara because you are finding out so much about your student, and he is finding out so much about you. You and he are coming alive to each other. You are demonstrating your willingness to see what is important to him, and he will begin to be willing to see what is important to you and eventually to *Hashem*.

Rabbi Horowitz writes, "In all my conversations with teenagers, the five words – uttered by youngsters with great bitterness and pain – that always render me speechless are, 'My parents don't know me.'"[32] Place this statement within the walls of a classroom, and it now reads, "My teachers don't know me." The consequences of this lack of knowledge can be disastrous.

For the teacher interested in the kind of self-revelation and student-revelation discussed so far, I found an extraordinary resource, Parker Palmer's *The Courage to Teach: Exploring the Inner Landscape of a Teacher's Life*. Palmer writes that the teaching life is filled with complexities that stem from three sources. "First, the subjects we teach

---

32 Horowitz, 2008, 59.

are as large and complex as life, so our knowledge of them is always flawed and partial... Second, the students we teach are larger than life and even more complex ... " Thirdly, "...we teach who we are."[33] The focus of Palmer's book is on the third reality, the one most often overlooked, that good teaching flows from the identity and integrity of the teacher. Writing with an uncommon honesty and compassion, Palmer helps any teacher see why he needs to face himself.

Rabbi Ginsburgh has much to say on this subject. He reminds us that one's ego is a barrier that stands in the way of seeing another person. If we are unaware or forgetful of this reality, we will go about projecting our own needs onto the other. To the extent that we do this, our efficacy in communicating with a student is very much reduced, and a negative spiral of disconnection may ensue. To salvage this situation, the Torah advises us to set aside specified times during the day/week for honest self-reflection. As we learn how to avoid our all-too-human inclination to selfishness and self-justification, we deepen our capacity for empathy, an empathy that comes from a place of humility. We are then in a position to influence another.[34]

On being able to influence others, the Lubavitcher Rebbe advises that although one must become involved with others, without delay, he must also "remember to work on his own development...

---

33 Palmer, 1998, 2.
34 See Part II, Chapters 1 and 6, *The Art of Education*.

Indeed, the correction of personal faults is as relevant to another as it is to oneself. For when one is deficient and neglects to correct his faults, the other will sense this and resist being influenced, and thus one cannot be as effective as one ought to be."[35]

Reb Simcha Wasserman tells us, "...the Master of the World has provided all of us with a degree of intuition as an automatic guide. It is especially strong in the area of child-raising... But this flow of intuition is dependent on one very important thing: that our concern is for the child and not for ourselves. Once we are concerned for ourselves, then there is no communication."[36]

Keep this insight from Reb Simcha Wasserman in front of you as we move into the chapter on testing. Testing by itself is not what bothers most of us. The problem is that when preparing for tests begins to dominate instruction, whether the tests are standardized or not, a change occurs, often unnoticed, in which we begin to define a student's needs in terms of his ability to pass a test. The reality is that his genuine needs as a young person and his ability to pass a test are most often not complementary. He may need to know how to pass a test; he may even feel more competent when he scores well, but again, it is a question of balance. If the mindset of testing predominates, the "flow of intuition" and the communication which could be available to us will weaken. All our

---

35 Schneerson, 1980, 154-155.
36 Branfman and Tatz, 1994, 71.

*Avoiding A March Through The Curriculum
With A Prescribed One-Size-Fits-All Method*

efforts to create responsive classrooms that promote connectedness will be thwarted unless we find less artificial ways for students to find out what they know, understand, and can do.

3
Confronting The Harmful Consequences Of The Present Uses Of Testing

Tests are commonplace tools. Examples of fairly straightforward ones are eye tests and tests of substances like water to find out whether or not a certain chemical is present. When a student takes a test, it is a way to find out – what? How many facts he has memorized? (At times, memorization is a useful skill.) How well he can apply his knowledge to a new situation? Which of his own ideas or inventions he can contribute to a subject? Which of his writings he thinks is his best and why? Where he ranks compared to others who are taking the same test?

Clearly, in the realm of testing a person's understanding of a topic or his ability to reason, the test design is not so simple as it is in the case of water content or the functioning of an eye. In the latter examples, there are agreed-upon procedures to guide the test design, specified data to be obtained, and unconflicted purposes for the tests. A human being, on the other hand, has a marvelous tendency not to fit into a universal descriptive "box." Testing people, therefore, becomes far more challenging. One medical doctor recently told me that high scores on professional tests do not guarantee fine doctors, and many doctors who are excellent in their fields do not score in the highest ranges. A medical technician related that though she was an excellent test taker, the standardized tests she took did not allow her to express what she could do best. Also, quite often she couldn't see the relevance of many of the test items.

The difficulties with testing people are numerous. One is the almost impossible task of removing the bias resulting from the test-maker's own culture and values. In addition, there is lack of agreement on at least four factors: the validity of tests (do they actually show what they purport to show?), the purposes of testing, the interests being served by testing, and the uses of test results. In spite of these difficulties, there is a fast-growing culture of testing that has made parents fearful that their child will have fewer and fewer chances to develop at a rate that suits him and eventually to reach a point of success. Many parents share the conviction that test results, by their very nature, offer only a limited glimpse of a student's capabilities; yet, because testing students from an early age onward has become pervasive, parents begin to surrender much of their judgment to test-makers who claim that by examining concrete test scores, parents will have an accurate picture of their child's strengths and weaknesses. If scores are high, parents are relieved that their child is bright and that his school is doing a good job. If scores are low, parents are relieved to find out early on that they need to look for specialists who can repair their child's deficiencies. Teachers are relieved that now they have "solid evidence" to support their "less than objective" assessments of a child, and school administrators are relieved to have "professional" records on every student which they can use to show parents that they and their staff have a concrete handle on each child's progress. It should be apparent that in this scenario, everyone's reasoning is starting from a flawed premise and can reach only flawed conclusions.

It is worth stating again that the information from tests, by the very nature of the way it is gathered, can represent only a tiny glimpse of a student's real capabilities, and this glimpse is momentary. It is true that most explanations of standardized tests are followed by disclaimers recounting their limitations. After including such disclaimers, many administrators and educators appear to be satisfied that they have made an honest statement about the imperfections of these tests and that teachers will view these tests in the same manner. Life moves on, the disclaimers recede into the background, and test results somehow become the predominant indicators of student and school performance.

I am urging that we find the courage within ourselves to face this phenomenon, identify the falseness that it contains, and revisit the decision to use standardized tests. At the very least, their use must advance the goal of responsive teaching. We must not be content to use them merely because of their nation-wide acceptance.

Two teachers described a testing experience with their students that shows how fleeting is the glimpse that a test affords. One test item asked a kindergartner to draw a shape that required him to cross the mid-line. He was unable to do it. A few days later, when the testing was over, his teacher watched him write an upper-case "I" and saw that he was crossing the mid-line easily. The second teacher gave her elementary students the Iowa test in early October. She received the results in late January of the following year. One of her students scored poorly in one of the sections of the test. By January, he had completely mastered the skills in this section. It is an accepted fact that the younger the child, the less conclusive many tests become. Even through high-school age, it is clear to me that test results receive far greater significance than they deserve, especially because instead of being used as possibly helpful feedback for an individual, they become, as one computer specialist described it, "a bureaucratic device to pigeon-hole people." Even with present statistical techniques, an accurate picture of an individual has yet to be produced from a test. It is hard to comprehend that in the face of the above-mentioned difficulties and the huge number of published writings which detail the limitations and the misuse of testing, our society is becoming more deeply immersed in the testing culture. This response is highly illogical. An extremely limited instrument has become accepted as an important resource for deciding the course of a child's future. This practice is not only illogical but also unethical.

Consider just one example, the experience of a tenth grader who moved from Mobile, Alabama, to Detroit, Michigan. She had been a strong "B" student. At her new school she had to take a standardized test to determine where she should be placed. The test results indicated that she needed a remedial class. She felt, and still feels to this day, that her placement was incorrect. After six months she was moved to a regular classroom. She is convinced that she could have performed well in the regular classroom from the beginning if the staff had given her the chance. Instead, for six months she had to work hard not to be defined by the less than desirable environment of this particular remedial classroom.

And remember Laura, the student who blossomed in Nancie Atwell's class? She had been tested at the beginning of second grade and placed in a low-track classroom for six years.

Yes, we must have ways to determine competency in professional fields, but the present uses of standardized tests in our schools do not promote the role of curriculum and instruction as a medium to respond to student needs. The reverse is the case. Teachers find themselves in the unenviable position of having to look at their students through "standardized glasses" in order to prepare them for tests that have come to represent significant gateways to opportunity or road blocks that deny it. The pressure is intense on both the teacher and the student. In 2003, a teacher in Buffalo, New York, wrote the following in her annual letter that she sends to family members: "We are teaching to new

New York State Regents exams this year, and they have changed in both topics covered and format quite a bit... For those of you unfamiliar with the Regents exams, the state gives an exam at the end of each class, specific to that particular class. So at the end of each class, kids all across the state take the same final exam for that class. The freshman math test is an especially high-stakes test, as they have to pass it to graduate from high school. As a teacher in New York State, it is a fact of life that you sell your soul to the Regents exams."

Later on in this letter, the teacher, now in the role of parent, writes, "Isaac is in the midst of the terrible two's... He is a very physical kid, with not much 'sit' in him. He is still slow at talking, however. He says a lot of individual words and some two-word phrases, but that's about it. We had him tested for speech therapy a week ago, and he qualified for the state early intervention program. [Soon] he will start getting speech therapy two times a week. Overall, we're not terribly worried – we are sure his speech will improve on its own. However, since the program is free through the state, we figured we would take advantage of it."

This mother is describing her two-year-old! I see a strong possibility that this parent-child relationship could become marred by the parent's hyper-alertness to any deviation from what is perceived to be the norm. We learn from psychologists that starting from birth, children respond to parental anxiety in ways that are counterproductive to healthy development. In all fairness to this mother, she may be trying to cover all the bases because as a teacher, she knows firsthand about the obstacle course her child will have to endure as he grows older. Every time a parent responds in this manner, however, he is reinforcing the testing culture, a culture which has been shown to work against the use of best education practices.

Angeline Lillard, an associate professor of psychology at the University of Virginia, develops this point in an article entitled "Testing Mania."[1] She reports that research suggests that the conditions created by emphasizing test performance as the accountability component impair teaching. At the very least, teachers who are worried about test scores are more likely to use forms of communication known to impact learning negatively. Worse still is the impact on teachers who are trying to improve their teaching practices; when such teachers are under pressure to produce high test scores, they find it extremely difficult to focus their energies on creating truly responsive classrooms. For most of us, the conditions that support risk-taking, reviewing how we teach, and making adjustments to meet the needs of our children simply do not exist in the climate of current testing practices.[2]

If this situation is bad for teachers, what happens to children? When our message to children is that doing well on a test is the main definition of success in school, children learn to consider test-taking as a kind of game. They pay attention to the information

---

 1   Lillard, 2004, 2.
 2   See "Getting Evaluation Wrong: The Case Against Standardized Testing," p. 73, in *The Schools Our Children Deserve* by Alfie Kohn.

they need to know for the test and disregard the rest. This attitude toward learning leaves little room for curiosity and reinforces the perception of school as something apart from one's real interests and concerns. Students also know that the way test results are used often causes them more harm than good. A high school student at Yeshiva Atlanta had this to say about her test scores: "I don't like to show my test scores to anyone else. If they scored higher than me, I'll feel bad. If I scored higher than them, they'll feel bad. My hope for the entire world is that there's no competition, because it messes everything up."[3] This student may not have supplied us with a carefully-reasoned argument, but we certainly get her point. She is alluding to her experience of school as a place where learning is an isolating activity in which she and her friends are pitted against each other to form a kind of pecking order. This ranking defines each student's standing by comparing his scores to those of the other test takers, a problematic procedure because it can offer only relative results. (These results can also be manipulated to produce higher scores.) To make matters worse, students feel keenly the anti-social repercussions of this grading system.

Obviously, this treatment of students and test results is harmful. It is harmful chiefly because it completely discounts the human being as the one creation who is capable of speaking. Rabbi Ginsburgh once again helps us here: "...what defines us as uniquely human is our ability to

---

3   *Atlanta Jewish Times*, Aug. 2, 1996, 12.

articulate our thoughts and feelings to other human beings... We have all experienced how talking things out, even to ourselves, helps us order and crystallize our thoughts. Often, articulating our thoughts helps us uncover deeper insights and perception into what we are articulating."[4] "If we have a positive idea, we want to express it in order to contribute to our own or others' well-being; if we have a problem, we want to air it in the hope that someone can help us resolve it."[5] Notice the relational aspect in all of Rabbi Ginsburgh's statements. Thus, when our high school student at Yeshiva Atlanta decried competition as messing everything up, she was expressing her frustration with the underlying disconnection, even opposition, brought about between herself and her friends and the resultant lack of opportunity for them to gain more focus and more clarification through dialogue as a regular part of their learning process. Competition in education requires a student to keep his advantage, so he feels compelled to horde information rather than to share it. Our student's frustration does have a positive component in that she is unwilling to accept the situation; she is not yet cynical.

    I remember several conversations among international students during the sixties when I was in graduate school. These students from countries around the world repeatedly commented, with much amazement on their faces, that American

---

4   Ginsburgh, 2002, 82.
5   Ibid., 56.

students would not share with them or their "fellow" Americans any information related to the studies they were all pursuing. Some forty years later, a Jewish student with a graduate degree in accounting told me about a "fellow" student who hid a particularly outstanding book so that no one else could use it.

The dean of a medical school at a large research university discovered that his students were exhibiting similar types of unethical behavior, such as cutting out a journal article assigned by a professor so that no one else could read it. He was also concerned to see other negative changes in his students as they progressed through the program towards graduation. When these students first entered medical school, they were motivated by a strong desire to help people return to good health. By graduation, the patient had become an object "to be repaired if possible and overlooked if not,"[6] and the student had become a player in an academic culture that emphasized besting one another in competition rather than learning in order to treat patients. Also, the emphasis on memorizing large collections of information left students with little time to develop the ability to find things out for themselves. They were not learning how to learn, a skill urgently needed in the medical profession, where the knowledge base is constantly expanding.

The dean actually turned this dismal situation around. On the first day of medical school, students

---

6   Palmer, 1998, 124.

were gathered in small circles around a live patient with a real problem. The students, supervised by a teaching physician, were asked to diagnose the patient's condition and prescribe a course of treatment. The physician's role was to guide a *collective* inquiry into the patient and the question of illness and health.[7] This small circle of students around a patient became "...the hub that turns a larger wheel."[8] Throughout their years in medical school, when these students engaged in research, seminars, and lab practice, they always returned to the hub – their small circle of peers around a live patient. They then moved out from the hub again with new questions.

The dissenting faculty was worried that standardized test scores would go down because no one was force-feeding students the facts. What actually happened? Not only did the medical ethics and bedside manner of the students improve but also the test scores actually started going up, and the dean reports that "...during the time we have been teaching this way, they have continued, slowly, to rise. In this approach to medical education, our students not only become more caring but also seem to be getting smarter, faster."[9]

The story of the change in this medical school is important for three reasons: first, it shows that when a student is focused on a vital center of his studies, in this case, the patient, he becomes

---

7 See *The Courage to Teach* for a discussion of the remarkable changes made by the dean, 124-128.
8 Ibid., 126.
9 Ibid., 127.

engaged. He is given the space to make a connection between himself, the patient, and the knowledge he needs to acquire. Secondly, when the student learns in cooperation with other students rather than in competition against them, his learning is significantly improved. Third, even when the emphasis is on connection and cooperation rather than "covering" vast amounts of information, the test scores rise. This result has been described in numerous studies, some of which I have included in this chapter. Even if students should later find themselves in competitive situations, they should be able to function well because their education was based on sound principles of how a person learns best.

Most of us tend to accept the notion that if we were all more alike, life would be easier. Of course, the fact is we are all different. How does the Torah view the amazing differences among people? Are these differences a hindrance, or should we be grateful for them? First of all, the Torah directs a person to be *receptive* to another rather than merely to tolerate him. A Jew needs to view the differentiating characteristics of others as a way to complete himself rather than to use these differences as sources of competition and strife. The Torah reality is that each Jew on his own is incomplete without the other, and this reality applies even if one is like the head in a human body and the other is like the leg.[10]

To gain even more of an understanding of how

---

10   Schneerson, 1999, 143.

competition in educational settings works against Torah values, see Chapter 6 in Alfie Kohn's book, *No Contest, the Case Against Competition.* Kohn's "Rx" for this devastating situation is not surprising; it is genuine cooperation, which happens to be a conspicuous piece of the structure in a differentiated classroom. Here, there is a much greater chance for students to have opportunities to work together daily, to share ideas and resources in small and large group gatherings, to take responsibility together for their classroom, and to evaluate themselves not only against specific examples of quality work which they see as they begin their activities but also against their own previous performance rather than that of their peers. It is important to know that Kohn cites evidence which shows that enhanced achievement and healthy self-esteem are more likely to result from working *with* other people rather than working *against* them.

In the previously mentioned article, "Testing Mania," Angeline Lillard gives two examples of studies that show that "…children do not actually learn better when there is an emphasis on test performance, even when those tests are of the everyday sort children routinely take in school."[11] Each study compared two groups of children. In the first study, students were given a short passage to read. One group was told that they would be tested on it "…to see if you're learning well enough." In the second group, the students were simply told that they would be asked questions about the

---

11   Lillard, 2004, 1.

passage. In the second study, the math performance of two groups of students was compared. The first group spent much time, over a three-year period, preparing for standardized tests. In the second group, little attention was paid to standardized tests, and, obviously, the teaching methods were quite different from those in the first group. In both studies, the children in situations where testing was not emphasized did better on conceptual learning, retention of facts and concepts learned initially, and application of knowledge. Amazingly, in the three-year study, the group of children who had been given open-ended problems which could be solved alone or in small groups did better on the standardized tests than their counterparts who had been drilled on procedures they would encounter on the tests.[12]

Lillard continues, "Children who had been learning in preparation for tests ... seemed to have 'inert' knowledge: they did not know how to apply their learning outside of the very specific context in which they had been taught. These and other studies indicate that learning in preparation for testing is superficial, inflexible, and not retained."[13]

---

12   See also the description of a study by Newmann, Bryk, and Nagaoka that examined the relationship of the nature of classroom assignments to standardized test performance, Tomlinson and McTighe, 2006, 176-177. The study concluded that "assignments calling for more authentic intellectual work actually improve student scores on conventional tests." The authors of the study define authentic intellectual work as "construction of knowledge, through the use of disciplined inquiry, to produce discourse, products, or performances that have value beyond school."

13   Lillard, 2004, 2.

Learning apparently is full of paradox. Many of us can remember having an assignment like reading a short story and being told at the outset that we will be tested on it. Somehow the fact that a test is coming disturbs the reading; the flow vanishes as we stop periodically to tell ourselves to remember this and to remember that. The direction of the story as it moves toward its high point becomes less vivid. The reader loses out on the wonderful interplay between his own personality and the emotions being evoked by the writer. There is a concern for someone else's agenda. Now imagine reading the short story because you chose it. You may know something about the author, or the title may have intrigued you. Your whole self is highly engaged as you read, and by the end of the story, you are awed by the author's talent. Now, as an afterthought, you are given a test on this story. Somehow your memory of the details is startlingly clear, and you have a keen grasp of the story's thrust.

I am certain that someone has studied this phenomenon and can explain it; suffice it to say for the moment that enough people have experienced this paradox for me to affirm its reality. In the meantime, people like Lillard have made the painstaking effort to show us in a more scientific manner that when we are allowed to draw on our internal motivation, we tap into a more potent energy, an energy that keeps pushing us beyond our present accomplishments.[14] The tapping of

---

14   Lillard, 2005, chapters 3 and 5.

this energy and the growth that accompanies it have all the characteristics of an optimal learning experience, exactly the type of experience that we desire for ourselves and for all our students. If we truly value this kind of learning, we have to find out which practices encourage it and which practices stifle it.

Before going further, I need to say that, within a context that respects best education practices, there is some room for testing as one among many ways to give students and teachers feedback. As stated earlier, the harm comes when performance on tests is used as the main measure of a student's accomplishments. When such tests are regularly used to compare students along a bell-shaped curve (norm-based grading), the results are misleading and certainly not helpful either to the strugglers or to the advanced learners![15] Lillard explains that under such conditions, a student tends to adopt performance goals rather than mastery goals;[16] i.e., he works for grades, not deeper conceptual learning that leads to a satisfying understanding of a subject.

Could it be useful at times to give a test but not attach a grade? Studies are showing that the very act of taking a test can help a student to focus more sharply, to process information more effectively, and to retain it longer, especially if the concern about a grade is absent.[17] Tests of this

---

15   Tomlinson and McTighe, 2006, chapter 8.
16   Lillard, 2005, chapter 5.
17   "Forget What You Know About Good Study Habits" by Benedict Carey, *The New York Times*, Sept. 6, 2010.

kind could be called practice tests or self-tests or feedback exercises. (I struggle to find the right term because the word "test" is loaded with negative associations.) Students could request this type of test when they are ready to find out what they know and what they need to revisit. By asking for such a test, a student is already taking a more active role in his own learning.

I asked a highly qualified mathematics teacher at a university for her opinion about the idea of giving students the chance to request a test. Without hesitation she answered that this practice is desirable and productive. She then told me that one year the head of her department approved a policy that teachers could not give any quizzes; only major tests were allowed. This policy was upsetting to her and to her students, who had heard from previous students how helpful these quizzes had been. One day four students approached the teacher and asked her please to give them quizzes. She thought about it and told them that when they were ready, they should come to her office during office hours, and she would give them a quiz. The usual time for taking these quizzes was about 15 minutes. When the students finished, the teacher examined the answers right away and explained whatever was incorrect in the solutions. Of course, no grades were recorded, and students continued coming to her office for quizzes throughout the semester. (The following semester, the policy of no quizzes was dropped.) This story shows how students themselves desired feedback on a regular basis, initiated a process to get it, and were fortunate enough to have a teacher who responded to their request.

Feedback from a quiz in any subject also helps teachers. In the conversations that ensue after the quiz, teachers have a chance to discover possible misunderstandings or gaps in communication between themselves and their students. Daniel Willingham, a cognitive scientist, writes, "When you think about it, how can you possibly improve unless there is some assessment of how you're doing? Without feedback, you don't know what changes will make you a better cognitive scientist, golfer, or teacher."[18] Another benefit is that a teacher can take note of a student who does not often request a test. Such a student may need additional or different instruction in order to build his self-confidence.

Tests used in this way are viewed as "helpers," not as "conclusive classifiers." Because this view is not common, teachers have the task of giving these exercises a positive connotation. If they have already taken steps toward more responsive teaching, this task will be easier. They can explain that the results of this kind of test will not be held against their students and that it is a genuine feedback exercise, much as a manufacturer gives his product a test run to see where it works and where it needs to be improved.

In a conversation with one of my piano students, I saw first-hand the power of the "test run." This

---

18   Willingham, 2009, 150.

student had asked to play at a "piano party" at my home. A piano party is a gathering of parents and friends who become the audience for a small number of my students. The students volunteer to perform, and they choose the music they want to play. My student selected three short pieces; she played them but was able to perform only one of them with real confidence. At her next lesson, sitting on the piano bench with a smile on her face, she offered to me the following words: "The minute I got home from the party, I sat down and practiced all the pieces I had played! And I'm going to practice more for the next party, and I'll do better." All this was said in her quiet but astute manner. I admire this nine-year-old, who could verbalize what she had learned from the experience of playing for an audience. Her "test run" had been successful.

Even the most constructive view of tests needs to be qualified. If we could imagine the best use of tests in education, we would still have to acknowledge that most of them are artificial. The testing situation cannot duplicate the conditions that would motivate a person in a real-life challenge. When one considers how many factors come into play when a person acts, that we cannot identify all of these factors for each person, and that these factors are likely to change over time, we have to conclude that a test, in the best of circumstances, is a limited instrument. It can tap into only a small part of the immense range of a person's capabilities. It has little power, therefore, to predict how successful a person will be. In the present testing culture, educators have to make an heroic effort to keep this perspective.

One of the characteristics of a well-functioning differentiated classroom is that responsibility for the quality of learning rests with both students and teacher. In this environment, opportunities for assessment occur daily and provide teacher and students with the data they need to adjust their strategies. The teacher typically posts in the classroom models and specific guidelines for evaluating quality, and these guidelines are stated in terms that are clear to the students. It is common to use rubrics, which are simple charts that present a continuum of achievement possibilities. As children become accustomed to this kind of environment, they can develop rubrics for themselves, with small pictures denoting, for example, the quality of the effort expended on a project. Thus, they become habited to stepping outside of their own activity and commenting on it; i.e., they become *metacognitive*. (Notice that this kind of thinking is very much related to the mind set developed by students of Gemara.)

Meanwhile, since students are learning to work more independently, the teacher can move about the classroom observing students as they work alone or in small groups. These teacher observations become invaluable moments for assessment. Since a teacher will often give a mini-lesson to three or four students, he has a good chance of seeing who understands and who doesn't. Even when the subject is math (perhaps, *especially* when the subject is math), a skilled teacher can guide whole-class and small group conversations which may reveal misconceptions and errors in thinking that otherwise are unlikely to surface. It is eye-opening to read actual conversations like these in the book, *Classroom Discussions: Using Math Talk to Help Students Learn.*

In addition, peer teaching becomes customary; it is structured clearly and has a good chance of being supportive since it is done in a non-competitive atmosphere. A student finds out immediately if he understands a concept when he attempts to explain it to a fellow classmate. Students become sources of information for each other, thus freeing the teacher even more to be able to observe his students and to make notes for necessary changes. Nancie Atwell gives a student the opportunity to ask his fellows to read his literary work and give him feedback. All of these practices require the ongoing creation of a genuine community of persons interested in each other's well-being. (Doesn't this sound like an "authoritative community?") I have been told that in such an atmosphere, students can often be harder on each other than their teacher might be! As long as their feedback is given in a community of reciprocal nurturing, they all stand a good chance of becoming living examples of the Torah's statement that each person needs the other to complete him.

Other ways to evaluate students' progress include examining students' products, going over students' journals, and reviewing questions which students use to indicate knowledge (or the lack of) about themselves in relation to a topic. Children have been asked to create portfolios of their finished work to show at parent-teacher conferences. In the video, "A Visit to a Differentiated Classroom," one hears the teacher talking with students about how to select what will go into a particular type of portfolio.

Tomlinson and McTighe have provided us with a sound, honest look at grading and reporting achievement in Chapter 8 of their book, *Integrating Differentiated Instruction and Understanding by Design*. This chapter and Chapter 5, in which the authors consider evidence of learning, give us a reasonable framework within which to consider questions like how can we maintain standards without standardization, how do assessments and testing differ, when to give a grade and when not to, how to make the information from grades clearer and more useful, and how to deal with the problematic nature of grades in general. Their discussion of feedback for the learner is exceptional. They suggest that for a feedback system to be effective, learners must be able to tell "...*specifically* from the given feedback what they have done well and what they could do next time to improve... Finally, the learner needs opportunities to act on the feedback – to refine, revise, practice, and retry."[19]

For obtaining specific feedback, teachers and students can benefit from the sensitive use of the video camera. I watched an elementary-aged student give a talk to his classmates. A videographer moved the camera back and forth between the student and his audience. After the

---

19   Tomlinson and McTighe, 2006, 77-79.

talk, the teacher and the student viewed the video together, and I could see that they were having an animated conversation. Each of them was probably sharing observations about such matters as how the speaker began, did this beginning grab his classmates and keep them interested, was he able to talk as if he were having a conversation with each of them, what were the expressions on his classmates' faces, did anyone appear to be drifting off, did he leave anything out which made it harder to follow his message, did he sound convincing, and did he seem to be enjoying himself. I am impressed with the wealth of information that can be extracted from a short video like this one. This exercise has an irresistible way of leading the student himself to discover ways to improve his ability to communicate to others. The video camera gives him extra eyes – a valuable service.

A word of caution: good practices, such as performance assessments and the use of rubrics, can be overdone. As noticed in the example above, about reading a short story and knowing in advance that you will be tested on it, a *preoccupation* with assessment "...can derail students' engagement with the learning itself."[20] Therefore, although assessment of students' learning is necessary and desirable, teachers must develop a sense for when to do it and when to refrain.

I have given only a brief description of some evaluation practices that promote learning. We need to study carefully these and other practices

---

20   Kohn, 1999, 196.

which are capable of giving teachers and students clearer feedback than the kind obtained from the standardized tests presently in use. Encouragingly, existing differentiated classrooms are already implementing alternative ways to evaluate student achievement, and these methods are supported by the available research on how children learn best.

These more useful methods build upon a common assumption – that the primary purpose of evaluating a student in any area is to help him become more competent as a learner, as an "interactor," and, in our case, as a Jew. It is not to "brand" him or to trick him, as one college student added when describing the multiple-choice tests he has had to navigate. When achievement tests or even the now commonplace personality and behavior questionnaires are used to compare a child to others of his age, educators must tread with extreme caution. I see at least two reasons for this caution. First, even the creators of nationally used tests are concerned that school administrators and government policy makers have taken a limited tool and run with it. This phenomenon is described in an article, "Experts: Student testing overdone."[21] In the article Steve Dunbar, head of Iowa Testing Programs, tells us that a consensus exists among test experts that a test is just a snapshot of where a particular child is on a particular day. These experts are also acknowledging other problems with high-stakes tests, including greater motivation to cheat and the possibility that results will be

---

21 *Atlanta Journal Constitution*, May 8, 2005, A1.

distorted by over-preparation. The second reason for caution is the growing pressure on kindergarten students to measure up to standards that are developmentally inappropriate. In *The Boston Globe*, Patti Hartigan writes that little children are being asked to perform academic tasks, including test taking, that early childhood researchers agree are not only inappropriate but potentially damaging.[22] Hartigan reports that often children are screened for kindergarten readiness even before school begins, and some are labeled "inadequate" or "not proficient" before they walk through the door. The result of this damaging trend is that very young children are already perceiving themselves as "kindergarten failures." On what grounds could anyone justify placing a child in this position? I cannot imagine any gain from this kind of treatment.

The antidote to this morass of malpractice is to remember that the Torah views the human being as the one creation who is capable of speaking. The human being speaks in order to relate better to himself and to others. This need to be connected to himself and to others is a primary need; as mentioned earlier, a Jew needs another to complete himself. On a global scale, this completion is what the Jewish people as a whole are working to attain, with *Hashem's* help. In this scheme, labels of "failure" make no sense. The completion which *Hashem* envisaged from the beginning of

---

22 "Pressure-cooker kindergarten," *The Boston Globe*, August 30, 2009.

His creation of the physical world cannot occur if one Jew is missing. There is no unimportant or useless Jew.

The chapter which follows will develop the differentiated classroom in more detail and will help us to see its immense possibilities – possibilities for the individual teacher, the individual student, and the teacher and students together as they create an optimal learning environment. In such an environment we should not be surprised to see signs of the eagerness, the delight, the attachment with which we started our lives at school; we may even see the best sign of all: a growing awareness of and connection to our *neshamas*.

4
Putting It All Together To Nurture A Paradigm Shift

Teachers are likely to teach the way they were taught. Many of their everyday actions and responses happen without thought. All of us operate this way; we are on "autopilot" most of the time until something novel comes our way that forces us to think. The challenge for teachers is that something novel is going to happen every day in their classrooms and, most probably, more than once as the day's events unfold. If a teacher wants to learn more about his students, he will see novel events in his classroom as opportunities, as clues which may lead to deeper insights into the way he and his students operate. This attitude means, however, that he will begin to question his automatic responses; in other words, he will have to think.

Thinking is not easy. It is not easy for teachers, and it is not easy for students. Daniel Willingham, whom I quoted in the chapter on testing, points out that thinking is slow, it takes effort, and the outcome is uncertain. In his book, *Why Don't Students Like*

School?, he tells us that, nevertheless, people will think if they perceive that their efforts will bring success. Most of us find pleasure in solving a problem. The problem, however, must be solvable; it must be at just the right level of difficulty – not too easy and not so hard that it seems overwhelming. The level has to be just a bit beyond what a person already knows and can do. Then the learner will be able to anticipate the pleasure of a successful outcome. The required effort will pay off. Teachers as learners have the job of finding this level of difficulty for themselves. When it is time to think, they must break down a particular challenge into manageable steps that allow them to be successful. The intent of this chapter is to make it easier for a teacher to find such steps.

Willingham considers teaching as an "act of persuasion;" the teacher is guiding students down a particular pathway and wants them to follow him. How does he persuade them to do this? Willingham answers that the teacher must keep his students interested; "to ensure their interest, you must anticipate their reactions; and to anticipate their reactions, you must know them."[1] This advice returns us to the theme of this book – connection. But Willingham doesn't stop here; a good teacher connects to his students but also must be able to organize the content of his lesson so that students will understand and remember.[2] The goal is to help students think about the meaning of a lesson.

---

1 Willingham, 2009, 162.
2 Ibid., 51.

One way to do this, writes Willingham, is to view to-be-learned material as a series of *answers*. The teacher should take the time to develop the questions because "it's the question that piques people's interest."[3] The question should be framed so that it will be engaging but not overwhelming and will take into account students' background knowledge. This powerful idea will be illustrated in the pages that follow. For now, I want to remind us of something we have always known – that the teacher plays a primary role in developing his curriculum. This truth prevails no matter what the school's philosophy may be.

It is worth restating Tomlinson's characteristics of a curriculum that is based on best education practices: it is important, focused, engaging, demanding, and scaffolded. We may ask, "Important to whom? Can a chapter in a textbook offer the kind of focus that is likely to absorb an individual? For whom is the curriculum engaging? Who is getting pushed to a higher level of understanding while being provided with the necessary support? Is part of one student's growth the result of hearing about the subject matter from another student's point of view? Does the student see value in the work for himself and for others?"

Implied in all of these questions is the presence of an individual student and his classmates. Educators know from experience that these students represent a wide range of readiness, interests, and abilities. If we want optimal learning environments for them,

---

3   Ibid., 16.

their presence must be the bottom-line reality for us. Their presence will actually become one of the greatest sources of the energy we are going to need to change. When a partner in any relationship can truly experience the presence of the other, both of them become more alive, and the possibilities for enhanced understanding in any area that the two of them are exploring are vastly increased.

In many schools, however, the definition of curriculum and the method of instruction prevent a teacher from utilizing the energy generated by student differences. The curriculum for a teacher most often consists of a list of objectives and state content standards and a textbook with a teacher's guide. The unstated assumption is that these materials are basically what the teacher needs. (In fact, these materials include more topics than he will be able to use.) Another unstated assumption is that the teacher's role is that of an expert administrator of someone else's creation. He doesn't feel empowered by this "gift" because he doesn't feel the sense of ownership that comes from participating in some way in the creation of the material and the stated priorities. Another difficulty is the fact that the textbook occupies such a central position. It may be an excellent textbook, but by the very way it is produced and by its purpose for being, it is not addressing anyone in particular! This is its nature. I am proposing that in an optimal learning environment, the textbook is simply one among many sources of information in a classroom – not the central one.[4] When the text is seen in this light, the need to cover it disappears. It is used when it can be helpful to the discussion at hand, like any other resource. It no longer blocks the teacher from experiencing the presence of a student, and the student is expected to ask his questions and seek his answers by consulting a variety of resources.

This view of the classroom requires the teacher to be more active in some areas and less active in others. He must frame his content and organize it since he is not relying on the textbook to do this for him. (The right frame can illuminate a picture; it literally throws a new light on an artist's work. By analogy, a teacher can frame content so that students gain a focus and a clarity that otherwise are unlikely to emerge. The topic of framing content will be developed in this chapter.) He must find out where his students are in relation to the content and how to present a topic so that it will intrigue them. He has to find ways to support his students, such as supplying needed vocabulary for some students and labeling resource materials with designations like "straight ahead," "uphill," and "mountainous," as one teacher did.[5]

On the other hand, students will gradually become more responsible for their work and its quality. In such a classroom, there is a drive for more independence and a sense of purposeful

---

4   See Tomlinson and McTighe, 2006, 28: "The textbook may very well provide an important resource, but it should *not* constitute the syllabus."

5   Ibid., 9.

energy coming from everyone. Problems don't produce an unnatural anxiety because students and teachers are accustomed to laying out options and exploring them. We all know that these kinds of skills are what our students will need for the rest of their lives. No one is saying that knowledge of specific subject areas is not important, but *the way* this knowledge is acquired can make the difference between someone who simply accumulates information and then forgets much of it and someone who continues to add to the knowledge he has because he is habited to building meaning upon meaning.

How, then, do we proceed? We have reviewed together the characteristics of a powerful curriculum, and we know that we must focus on whom we teach and how we teach. As mentioned earlier, now the teacher is the one who must frame and organize his content. He is the one who must develop ongoing ways to know his students and use this information when planning instruction. And he is the one who will need assessment tools to find out how well his instruction is working and where it may need adjusting. Two expert educators, Carol Ann Tomlinson and Jay McTighe, decided to work with each other to give teachers the tools they need. In their book, *Integrating Differentiated Instruction and Understanding by Design*, they have provided not only a way of thinking but also concrete examples, strategies for teachers to get started, a list of resources (including their e-mail addresses), and an actual unit plan which incorporates differentiated instruction and understanding by design.

Before I describe their efforts, I want to share with you an interesting observation. Good teachers have often intuitively understood their students' needs, crafted positive responses to these needs, and shaped their curricula into powerful vehicles for learning. Many of us have watched such teachers and are awed by the way they seem to possess an extra sense when it comes to understanding their students, motivating them, or supplying them with a missing link that they need in order to move forward. People often say that such teachers have a knack for their work. Even if it is true that some people have innate characteristics that contribute to their success as teachers, I strongly suspect that the chief ingredients in their success are their *interest* in how children learn and their *will* to pursue this interest until they can act on it. One principal, Deborah Meier, upon being told that her faculty was remarkable, explained that her school's staff "...is not remarkable because they are more gifted than other teachers or because they have taught longer or because they went to more exclusive colleges. They are remarkable, says Meier, because they live what they believe."[6]

We Jews are on the receiving end of a long line of ancestors who lived what they believed. In a literal sense, we inherit from them this ability. I am assuming, therefore, that we have a significant number of "remarkable" teachers in Jewish schools – teachers who are interested in how children learn and who will pursue this interest to the point

---

6   Tomlinson, 2003, 26.

of taking action if they will persist in defining themselves as professionals. One characteristic of a professional is that he networks with experts in his field. The remainder of this chapter is my attempt to network with Carol Ann Tomlinson and Jay McTighe. Like good teachers, they are demanding. They remind us that our own improvement will occur only if we are willing to leave our comfort zones, take risks, reflect, and adjust. These are large demands; therefore, the authors are quick to give us the support we need to ensure success for our students and, thereby, to achieve our own success as teachers.

Tomlinson and McTighe understood the necessity to make explicit the intuitive understandings of great teachers. Tomlinson had worked on the elements of differentiated instruction; McTighe had worked on the design of powerful curriculum. Through a series of meetings with each other and with other colleagues, they came to see that each approach needs the other in order to accomplish the goal they both were seeking – high-quality learning for everyone. The result of their collaboration is the above-mentioned book, *Integrating Differentiated Instruction and Understanding by Design.*

These authors were seeking answers to the following questions: How can I, the teacher, design a worthy curriculum that will connect to all of the students in my class? How will I know that my students have understood the big ideas I presented? How will I know that my students are acquiring knowledge and skills as a result of their work in a given topic?

Notice that Tomlinson and McTighe began their exploration of high-quality teaching and learning by posing questions for themselves. Questions focus an investigator's attention. They act like magnets, attracting the information that will help to uncover answers. Just as questions help adult researchers, our authors understood that questions are powerful tools for students.[7]

Tomlinson and McTighe suggest that the first step in designing a worthy curriculum is to select from the subject matter a big idea, also termed an enduring understanding. A teacher must ask himself what is truly worthwhile to learn from a given topic. How will my students gain power from learning this? For each topic to be presented, Tomlinson and McTighe propose that a teacher select one or two big ideas and related essential questions that are designed to arouse the curiosity of his students. They suggest that teachers meet together to tease out these understandings and questions. Many examples are already available both in their book and on the UbD (Understanding by Design) Exchange website.[8] This website contains a large number of unit designs in UbD format and "Web links for finding 'big ideas,' essential questions, performance assessment tasks, and rubrics. It makes no sense to reinvent the wheel."[9]

---

    7   Remember Willingham's advice to teachers to take the time to develop questions for their students. It was a pleasure to see a meeting of the minds of Tomlinson, McTighe, and Willingham on the subject of questions as powerful tools.

    8   http://ubdexchange.org

    9   Tomlinson and McTighe, 2006, 32.

Identifying enduring understandings and essential questions is the first stage in the three-stage backward design process for curriculum planning. Once these goals are clarified, Tomlinson and McTighe lead us to the second stage: considering *"in advance* the assessment evidence needed to document and validate that the targeted learning has been achieved."[10] Finally, with clear goals and assessment tools in mind, the teacher has reached the third stage: planning purposeful learning experiences and instruction which "help *all* students reach the desired achievements."[11]

Tomlinson and McTighe describe two enduring understandings selected by a teacher, a Ms. Kanefsky, to introduce her third graders to the period in U.S. history when people living on the east coast began moving westward. The teacher's two understandings were that change involves risk and that change can be both positive and negative. As part of the unit pre-assessment (which was not graded), Ms. Kanefsky asked her students to write or draw about "(1) a change in their lives or in the life of a family member that involved a move or taking a risk and (2) an example from history when change had been positive and when it had been negative."[12] Through this pre-assessment the teacher found out quickly who could or could not relate well to the unit's enduring understandings. She also had a way to begin connecting classroom discussions about westward migration with the

---
10 Ibid., 28.
11 Ibid., 29.
12 Ibid., 43.

students' own experiences.[13]

Later in the unit she involved all students in making a simulated journey west. For students who were more concrete in their thinking, she asked them to write a series of letters to a person "back home," in which they talked about the risks they encountered and the positives and negatives they experienced. Students who could operate at a more abstract level wrote reflective diaries examining both events and their thoughts about the events. Students with mild retardation created, with their teacher's help, a trip quilt that showed the enduring understandings in visual images![14] Students often shared their work with the other groups and with the whole class and, thus, were able to benefit from the work of their peers.

Tomlinson and McTighe offer many beautiful examples like this one and also present, in detail, an entire unit plan for fifth or sixth graders on nutrition. The plan follows clearly the three stages of the backward design process and illustrates ways to differentiate the unit.[15] Studying this unit plan will reveal to you the kind of thinking that makes curricula come alive. For now, I do want to share with you the essential questions for this unit that were developed to hook students: "What is healthful eating? To what extent are you a healthful eater? Could a healthy diet for one person be unhealthy for another? Why do so many people have health problems caused by poor nutrition despite all of the

---

13   Ibid.
14   Ibid.
15   Ibid., 144-162.

available information about healthful eating?"[16]

In Chapter 7 of Tomlinson and McTighe's book is a section entitled "Using Essential Questions in Teaching." If you are short on time, be sure not to miss pages 110-116. Like Willingham, the authors ask us an essential question about content, any content, that goes like this: "If the content we study represents the 'answers,' then what were the questions?" The authors then give us an example from a course on U.S. government. Instead of requiring students to memorize the three branches of government and their functions, the teacher can introduce the content via questions like the following: "What might happen if people become too powerful? How might a country (or state) keep government leaders from abusing their power? Are there ways that power can be controlled?"[17] The goal is to help students understand that the three branches of government, two Houses of Congress, etc., are "answers" to these questions. These questions also give students a way to look at "solutions" created by other nations. Framing the content in this manner does, indeed, make the students in this class more powerful by giving them a way of thinking that is broad enough to be applied in other contexts.

I was also excited by the idea in this section that essential questions are meant to be revisited. They are posed at the beginning of a unit, can be considered again midway through the unit,

---

16   Ibid., 147.
17   Ibid., 111.

and then can be discussed once more at the end. Thus, essential questions become not only a way to uncover content but also a way to assess understanding over time.

Remember Rabbi Ginsburgh's words, quoted in the Preface: "The wisdom of the Torah can identify what is true and what is not in secular inquiry, and associate each truth with its appropriate context in the Torah's own world-view." Would the Torah consider Tomlinson and McTighe's use of essential questions as a "truthful" way to introduce content to students? We could ask ourselves, "Do Jews encounter the use of essential questions in the Torah?" Rabbi Ginsburgh points out a place dear to all of us: the Passover Haggadah.[18] He sees the Haggadah as a source from our sages of "specific techniques of communication that relate to education..."[19] The story that it tells begins with the Four Questions. Rabbi Ginsburgh derives from this order that "a teacher should construct his lesson plan in a manner that encourages students to ask questions. Students should ideally be able to come up with the questions themselves, but if they do not, it is up to the teacher to bring them up."[20] What kinds of questions are most effective for students' growth? He answers that a teacher should "...try to peak the students' interest by asking questions that require thought and analysis to answer."[21]

And remember Tomlinson's requirement that

---

18 Ginsburgh, 2005, 166-169.
19 Ibid., 166.
20 Ibid., 168.
21 Ibid.

curriculum be engaging? This characteristic is emphasized in the Haggadah by its insisting that each one of us must consider himself as though he came out of Egypt and that if G-d had not taken us out, we and our children would still be slaves to Pharaoh. Rabbi Ginsburgh translates these messages into educational practices with the following: "This teaches the importance of focusing on the practical implications of an idea and demonstrating how it concretely affects the student's life."[22]

Even the process of starting with the end result (big ideas or enduring understandings) and planning backwards can be seen as an earthly expression of the manner in which *Hashem* created the physical world. "God began by formulating a vision of the possible perfected state of the universe as it will be in the future ... It was this final vision that actually inspired and guided the subsequent acts of creation. This is similar to our own creative process where we first visualize the finished product, hold it in our mind's eye, and try to project that image onto the physical world."[23]

Thinking of big ideas and then planning backwards may not be easy at first. If this process is new to us, it may be hard to get started, and we may not be convinced of the advantages of this way of planning. It is important, therefore, to communicate with teachers who have become experienced with backward design and to consider three advantages

---

22   Ibid., 168-169.
23   Ibid., 72.

that Tomlinson and McTighe feel are compelling. One advantage is that it avoids the problem of offering students experiences and activities that may be interesting and hands-on but that don't lead anywhere because they weren't planned within a goal-oriented context. Another problem that can be avoided is the pressure to cover a large amount of material with never enough time. The enduring understandings and essential questions help to sort out material which is relevant and encourage students to probe more deeply into a given subject. The third advantage is that clarity about essential outcomes makes differentiation possible. "In an effectively differentiated classroom, the same powerful understanding-based goals will nearly always 'belong' to everyone."[24] Thus, no one is "dumbed down." Each student works with the big ideas of a unit at a level of complexity appropriate to him.

Let us look for a moment at one aspect of the Judaic curriculum through the lens of differentiated instruction and understanding by design. One important skill that students need to acquire is the ability to read biblical Hebrew. Let us assume that we have teachers who are familiar with the processes of differentiated instruction and understanding by design. One of their first steps would probably be to organize a meeting for the purpose of brainstorming ways to make the learning of biblical Hebrew more engaging and meaningful for each student. Someone at this meeting might

---

24   Tomlinson and McTighe, 2006, 41.

suggest that the teachers work together to come up with an enduring understanding or two and some essential questions about the Hebrew language. Here are some questions that occurred to me: Where do the words I use every day come from? Have English letters always looked the way they look today? Was there a time when language didn't exist? Did the Hebrew language start the same way that other languages started? These questions might stimulate a teacher to ask, "What do we really want our students to understand about the Hebrew language?" A colleague might reply, "The Hebrew language is unique and has a power that no other language has. Could this be an enduring understanding?" The conversation might continue with more stimulating ideas like the following: The world was created with Hebrew letters. *Hashem spoke* the world into existence. Actually He *speaks* the world into existence. What difference does it make for our students that the world is created in this fashion?

This meeting could be a forum for teachers to share previous experiences that relate to the topic. An example is an actual experience at a workshop on Jewish education where a teacher met a *morah* who had taught young children for many years. This *morah*, one of the presenters at the workshop, had made many games with Hebrew letter cards, but she told everyone that she never puts these cards directly onto the floor because the letters are holy. The teacher who is recalling this workshop could ask her colleagues to imagine the impact this must have had on the children of this *morah*.

She adds, "I think this one practice makes such a powerful statement that the children in this class most likely will not have forgotten it. It certainly remained with me."

The point of my creating this imagined meeting with Judaic teachers is to convey the richness that is possible when professionals with a common aim sit down together to probe and question until they arrive at big ideas and essential questions that vitalize their curriculum. All beginnings are difficult, but if these meetings become habitual, I predict that ideas will begin to flow with greater ease as teachers come to the table with more and more successes behind them. As they become more comfortable with this process, it is quite possible that they will offer their students chances to formulate essential questions. When students originate these kinds of questions, they are truly engaged. To paraphrase Alfie Kohn, students learn to ask good questions by asking questions.[25] And just as in the case with teachers, students become more effective when they can try out their questions in a group setting.

Tomlinson and McTighe point out that there are several misunderstandings about how people learn which could hold teachers back from fully embracing the idea of teaching for understanding and responsive instruction. One of these misunderstandings is the notion that a person must acquire requisite skills and facts *before* he can be expected to understand more abstract ideas and

---

25   Kohn, 1999, 151.

apply them in an authentic context.[26] The authors state that this notion is at odds with contemporary views of the learning process. The contemporary view is that "through the interplay of drill and practice in combination with authentic tasks," a person gains understanding and is able to transfer his knowledge to new contexts. It is actually through being challenged to apply his learning that a person comes to see the need for "basic skills." Otherwise, as Tomlinson and McTighe explain, it is like a baseball player who is always practicing a skill on the sidelines but never gets to play the game. Denzel Washington, an Oscar-winning actor and director, came at this idea from another angle: "...you don't realize what you know until it's time to apply."[27]

Another misunderstanding is the notion that differentiation means making an individual plan for each student. Tomlinson and McTighe state clearly that this is not feasible. Responsive teaching calls for the teacher to implement *patterns* of instruction that are likely to serve multiple needs.[28] These authors then list ten teaching patterns that "cut across 'categories' of students and benefit academic success for many learners."[29] By using these patterns, a teacher can become more aware of individual learners, even though he may not be accomplishing this awareness on a one-by-one basis, a task which would be well-nigh impossible.

---

26   Tomlinson and McTighe, 2006, 119.
27   *Wall Street Journal*, Dec. 22-23, 2007, W2.
28   Tomlinson and McTighe, 2006, 19.
29   Ibid., 20ff.

Here are a few of the suggested patterns:

~ Find ways to get to know students more intentionally and regularly.
~ Incorporate small-group teaching into daily or weekly teaching routines.
~ Learn to teach to the high end. (Once again, remember Laura, the student in Atwell's writing and reading workshop.)
~ Offer more ways to explore and express learning.
~ Allow working alone or with peers.
~ Use clear rubrics that coach for quality.

Related to using patterns of instruction is the idea of clustering learner needs to make instructional planning more efficient.[30] Tomlinson and McTighe explain this clustering approach with an analogy from the field of architecture. Architects are now required to provide access to buildings for people who are handicapped. The common solution is to build a ramp. What has transpired is that the ramp has become useful not only to people in wheelchairs but also to parents with babies in strollers, people with rolling suitcases, and delivery people with carts or dollies. The authors continue, "…it's almost certain that a 'ramp' we think we are building for one student or one group of students would be of great help to others as well."[31] Returning to the architect's domain, we would agree that it is far

---
30 Ibid., 94ff.
31 Ibid., 96.

easier to build a ramp while a building is under construction than to install one in an already finished structure. Likewise, teachers must do a kind of "anticipatory" planning and think in terms of addressing patterns of student need and strength "...as part of classroom routines rather than as interruptions to classroom routines..."[32] Since a picture is worth a thousand words, it would be useful to view the video, "Instructional Strategies for the Differentiated Classroom," available from the Association for Supervision and Curriculum Development.

The last point is not so much a misunderstanding as it is a worry. Teachers worry that if they allow time to explore a topic in depth, their students will lose out by not covering enough of the curriculum. This view dies hard, but it flies in the face of present research in cognitive psychology. Tomlinson and McTighe report key findings from a book, *How People Learn: Brain, Mind, Experience, and School*.[33] One of these findings is the following: "Research on expertise suggests that superficial coverage of many topics in the domain may be a poor way to help students develop the competencies that will prepare them for future learning and work. Curricula that emphasize breadth of knowledge may prevent effective organization of knowledge because there is not enough time to learn anything in depth. Curricula that are 'a mile wide and an inch deep' run the risk of developing disconnected

---

32   Ibid.
33   Bransford, Brown, and Cocking, 2000.

rather than connected knowledge."³⁴

Here is another interesting finding from an exhaustive analysis of classroom teaching in the United States, Japan, and Germany. In this study the researchers "present striking evidence of the benefits of teaching for understanding in optimizing performance."³⁵ For example, data from various studies clearly show that "although the Japanese teach fewer topics in mathematics, their students achieve better results."³⁶ Tomlinson and McTighe summarize these findings with the following words: "...nations with higher test scores use teaching and learning strategies that promote understanding rather than 'coverage' and rote learning."³⁷

Perhaps it is easier now to understand the different role I am urging for the textbook. Its presence is good when it is one among many resources that contribute to the goals of a responsive classroom. In the light of this view, it is important for us to be aware that publishers are offering textbooks with computer components for teachers and students. These components have the capability of giving a teacher choices among several levels of text, lesson plans, and materials. These programs can write a test for a teacher. They can also simulate actual laboratory activities in a science unit. The student can find his textbook online and can use this accessibility in a number of ways, including

---

34   Tomlinson and McTighe, 2006, 174.
35   Ibid., 177.
36   Ibid., 177-178.
37   Ibid.

printing question-answer activities from the book and then writing answers on this sheet.

It is safe to predict that more and more computer-based learning activities will be designed for students at every grade level. With each advance in technology, however, educators need even more to be able to discern whether such activities do, in fact, enhance a student's understanding. We have all experienced the distortion of a well-intended innovation; the only way to prevent negative outcomes from new materials is to make sure that we can justify their use in an understandings-based curriculum. For example, whenever a textbook offers a teacher different levels of instruction, the teacher must examine these levels carefully to see if they measure up to the demands of the responsive teaching model we have been discussing. In other words, the teacher must ask himself if the activities at each level present meaningful, significant problems or projects for each student. It is too easy to fall once again into the trap of assigning unchallenging, unimportant work to a student who, for example, has difficulty with the English language or who has less experience with the topic at hand. The textbook, with all its computer-generated possibilities, is like the proverbial ax. It is the teacher who is the wood-chopper. The ax may be sharp, but its efficacy still depends upon the wood-chopper.

One further point needs mentioning here. An optimal learning environment is for teachers as well as students. Teachers continue learning. Students need to see their teachers thinking, pondering, questioning, reading, creating, becoming excited about their own or someone else's discoveries, and, perhaps most importantly, dealing with a failure or a disappointment. Students need to see their teachers as human beings who struggle and who are courageous and who deeply care about them. With all our concerns about curricula and the recent advances in transmitting information around our globe, we can easily forget that the daily actions of teachers who are creating responsive classrooms may be among the lasting impressions our students take with them.

We have lifted our sights. We have seen alternatives that promise so much more than our present practices. We may be inspired, but the question remains: How do we get going? The following steps are a result of my thoughts together with the advice of Tomlinson and McTighe.

The first step is for a teacher to be hooked on the idea of designing a meaningful curriculum for his students and differentiating his instruction. The way to become hooked is to read as much as possible about these ideas, to network with people using these ideas, and to see these ideas in action by viewing available videos. The heads of schools must become hooked, also. One of their functions has always been to reflect on the current learning environments in their schools and to encourage adjustments that may be needed in the light of research on how students learn best. Just as students need to be supported when they leave their comfort zones, teachers need this support from their principals.

The next step is to select one or two possible changes from a list of indicators of optimal learning environments. (I use "indicators of optimal learning environments" and "best education practices" interchangeably.) It is important that a teacher select a change that is highly appealing to him so that he will persist in his efforts over a period of time. Again, just as a student is motivated by success, so, too, is a teacher. It has been my experience that if a teacher sees even one of his students beginning to change into a more thoughtful, reflective person, this happy event will feed the teacher's desire to continue working toward his chosen goals.

Here is an example of a change that could be made to empower a student to see himself as an editor. What often happens at present is that a student turns in a project and receives a grade on it. He may have been given a list of requirements for the project, but the list usually doesn't show him how to evaluate himself as he goes along. After the grade has been given and if the teacher finds the time, he may discuss the weak points of the project with the student and encourage him to do better on the *next* project. This is not a good educational practice. The student needs, from the beginning, a way to judge how he is doing and opportunities all along the way to get feed-back from his peers and teacher. When he is finished with what should be considered his first draft, he needs time to revise it, not wait for the next project. He needs the opportunity to follow through with improvements on his current project until he is satisfied that he has done his best to meet the specific descriptions of high quality work that were posted in his classroom at the beginning of the assignment. When a student goes through this process, he truly will have gained skills he can use in his next project, and his success will give his teacher the energy to keep selecting more and more changes.

Now we need to see a list of indicators of optimal learning environments. Tomlinson and McTighe offer one. It is divided into four categories: the learning environment, the curriculum, the teacher, and the learners. Within each category there are at least seven descriptions.[38] I have selected a few of these to share with you: "There is a balanced emphasis on individuals and the group as a whole. Students work together collaboratively. All students have respectful work – that is, tasks and assessments focused on what matters most in the curriculum, tasks structured to necessitate high-level thinking, and tasks that are equally appealing and engaging to learners. Assessment of understanding is anchored by 'authentic' performance tasks calling for students to demonstrate their understanding through application and explanation. The unit or course design enables students to revisit and rethink important ideas to deepen their understanding. The teacher and students use a variety of resources. The teacher helps students connect the big ideas and essential questions of the unit with their backgrounds, interests, and aspirations. The teacher facilitates students' active construction of meaning, rather than simply 'telling.' The

---

38   Ibid., 162ff.

teacher understands that individual learners will make meaning in different ways and on different timetables. The teacher uses questioning, probing, and feedback to encourage learners to 'unpack their thinking,' reflect, and rethink. Students are engaged in activities that help them learn the big ideas and answer the essential questions. The teacher provides meaningful feedback to parents and students about students' achievement, progress, and work habits. Students can explain what they are doing and why (i.e., how today's work relates to the larger goals). Students contribute actively to effective functioning of classroom routines and share responsibility with the teacher for making the class work. Students regularly reflect on and set goals related to their achievement, progress, and work habits."

These are impressive indicators. In addition, you, as a teacher, will likely bring into your classroom your own unique set of personal goals. To get started, you have to decide which change is calling the loudest to you at the moment. Look upon your decisions as a way of creating, step by step, a new culture within your school. Keep a journal to record and review conversations with yourself. Always look for one or more colleagues with whom to plan and problem-solve, and remember to partner with specialists. Lastly, don't underestimate your successes, no matter how small you think they are. I like to remember that infants and toddlers don't stop when their countless daily efforts to acquire new skills and understandings don't always seem to work out. They persist, and then they persist again. Adults always marvel at their energy; perhaps one of the reasons they have it is to be able to persist in this fashion. If we, as adults, can recapture this kind of drive, which is complex and, at the same time, so simple, we will have the strength to create the learning environments that our students deserve.

5
Words Of Encouragement

"A single act is better
than a thousand groans."[1]

One of the purposes of this book was to identify three practices that stand in the way of creating optimal learning environments. By now, many of us may have noticed that these practices are intertwined with each other; therefore, when you start anywhere in this tangled web, you will affect another practice. If you have a difficult student, make the choice that you are going to do something with him to get to know him better. You may have to show extreme sensitivity, and you may have to persist over time. When you uncover a positive attribute of his, consider this discovery a real victory. You will look for more, and then you notice that you are looking at other children differently. You begin to change the tasks you had planned for this student. (At least for him, the curriculum is becoming responsive.) You are keeping anecdotal observations and

---

1   *Hayom Yom, Adar Sheini* 8, 35.

possibly a portfolio about him. You are collecting information from his other teachers and reflecting on it together. Now, if you are forced to give him a standardized test, this test truly becomes only one part of a much larger description and unfolding of this student. Now you have a context in which you can decide whether or not the weaknesses that appear on his test can be useful as feedback. At the very least, the test results won't be used as indicators of intractable deficiencies.

Angeline Lillard discusses two models of American education adopted at the turn of the twentieth century: the school as a factory and the child as a blank slate. Though we all know rationally that these models were never sound, "…they continue to have a profound impact on how schooling is done."[2] It is quite stimulating (and disturbing) to read her entire discussion of the influence of these models. She concludes that "…the evidence from psychological research suggests truly radical change is needed…," not just a new reading program here or a new technique there.[3] She is pushing for deeper change, with more accurate models of the child and the school.

We Jews, radical as our tradition has always been, possess accurate models of the child and the school. When *Hashem* gave us His Torah, He supplied us with a model of the child and of the learning process that is entirely different from that which took hold in America. Children, rather

---

2   Lillard, 2005, 3.
3   Ibid., 15, 16.

than being regarded as blank slates, are the purest and the closest ones to the essence of Torah. As stated previously in this book, each Jew is given a unique combination of characteristics; his teachers, therefore, must "... guide, train, dedicate ... whatever he has *brought with him* in the way of talents and capabilities for the life which lies before him."[4] (italics mine) Moreover, since every Jew comes into this world equipped with a *neshama*, which is a part of *Hashem* Himself, he has the most powerful generator of wisdom, understanding, and knowledge that one can possibly possess. And for Jews, the learning process throughout the ages has been an active model rather than the passive model of the factory, where children are given the same information at the same time and are moved from one place to another when a bell rings. The success of a factory depends upon ensuring that all items of a given model conform to the same specifications. Contrast this conception of education with that of the Lubavitcher Rebbe: "Each person possesses a particular virtue in which he surpasses all others, even the leaders of the generation. He (and those who help him in his growth and development) should not seek universal conformity, but should strive to cultivate this unique gift."[5]

Our great Torah leaders have always directed our attention to every individual's potential for growth and to the need to take into account all of a person's "...talents and aptitudes, his way of thinking, his

---

4   Hirsch, 1976, 125.
5   Touger, 1994, 53.

sensibilities and his feelings, his wishes and his motivations, his talk and his actions."[6] They are relentless in their emphasis on a student's need for colleagues, the value of asking questions and engaging in lively dialogue, the necessity for review (even one hundred and one times), the advantages gained when a person can extend his knowledge into new and different settings, the value of each student's perspective, and the profound respect, even love, between a rebbe and his student that constitutes the foundation for their being able to learn together.

All of these are elements of quality education, and they originate in the Torah. I am excited that those who are studying human development have found their way to these truths within the perspective of their own professions. Though not illuminated by Torah, the research that Lillard assembled, the studies described by Tomlinson and McTighe, and the guidelines that they and others are developing for creating differentiated instruction do have the ability to assist us in bringing our own cherished ideals down to earth. When teachers benefit in this way, they are also empowered to transform themselves, and, if I may extend Vivian Gussin Paley's observation, everyone in these classrooms rises in stature.

Furthermore, we Jews have a powerful advantage in this work of changing. We have our father, Avraham, who refused to conform, who constructed himself anew ten times, and who invited everybody

---

6   Hirsch, 1976, 126.

in. The translation of Avraham's attributes into education might sound like this: the teacher welcomes and values every student and offers him safety. In the interplay between himself and his student, he remakes himself continually.

We inherit not only Avraham's confident outwardness but also Yitzchak's rich inwardness. In educational terms, the teacher reflects. He digs deeply, as Yitzchak dug wells, to unearth elements in his own and his students' personalities and to find enduring understandings and essential questions for his students. He also perceives when it is best for him to step aside, to hold back so that his student can receive what is being offered and not feel overwhelmed.

In building our new structure we have yet another resource – Yaakov's attribute of *tiferes*, translated as beauty or harmony or truth. Our sages explain that beauty comes from a fusion of the attributes of Avraham and Yitzchak. "For neither a single motif, nor its opposite, is beautiful. Beauty comes from the fusing of different and even opposite tendencies."[7] So, also, Yaakov is identified with the quality of Truth. "...Truth has a dimension that transcends mortal limits, being above all possibility of change or interruption. With Truth, one can reach out and change environments, for nothing can oppose Truth."[8] How do we bring our inheritance from Yaakov into our schools? The teacher will see beauty in his classroom when

---

7   *In the Garden of the Torah*, 1994, Vol. I, 42.
8   Ibid., 43.

a student has been able to harness the different tendencies within himself for a positive end and when the class as a whole has benefited from the differences among its members.

It follows, then, that just as a good teacher pushes a student slightly beyond his present capabilities while providing the needed support, we can reach very much beyond our present practices in schools because we have a "scaffolding" that is timeless. Armed with this scaffolding, a Jew does not have to calculate. He can just begin.

References

Armstrong, Thomas. (2000). *In Their Own Way.* New York: Penguin Putnam.

Atwell, Nancie. (1991). *Side by Side: Essays on Teaching to Learn.* Portsmouth, NH: Heinemann.

_____. (2007). *The Reading Zone.* New York, NY: Scholastic, Inc.

Branfman, Yaakov and Tatz, Akiva. (1994). *Reb Simcha Speaks.* Brooklyn, NY: Mesorah Publications, Ltd.

Chapin, Suzanne H.; O'Connor, Catherine; and Anderson, Nancy Canavan. (2003). *Classroom Discussions: Using Math Talk to Help Students Learn.* Sausalito, CA: Math Solutions Publications.

Eisemann, Rabbi Moshe M. *Worlds Beneath the Word: Mining Pirkei Avos for Chinuch Insights.*

Ginsburgh, Rabbi Yitzchak. (2002). *Transforming Darkness into Light: Kabbalah and Psychology.* Jerusalem, Israel: Linda Pinsky Publications, a division of Gal Einai.

_____. (2005). *The Art of Education: Internalizing Ever-New Horizons.* Jerusalem, Israel: Gal Einai.

Goertz, Donna Bryant. (2001). *Children Who Are Not Yet Peaceful.* Berkeley, CA: Frog, Ltd.

Goldberg, Rabbi Hillel. (1992). *Illuminating the Generations.* Brooklyn, NY: Mesorah Publications, Ltd.

Goleman, Daniel. (2006). *Social Intelligence: The New Science of Human Relationships.* New York, NY: Bantam Dell.

Halasz, George; Anaf, Gil; Ellingsen, Peter; Manne, Anne; and Salo, Frances Thomson. (2002). *Cries*

Unheard: A New Look at Attention Deficit Hyperactivity Disorder. Altona, Victoria, Australia: Common Ground Publishing.

Hardwired to Connect: The New Scientific Case for Authoritative Communities. (2003). New York, NY: Institute for American Values.

Hirsch, Rabbi Samson Raphael. (1976). *From the Wisdom of Mishle*. Jerusalem and New York: Feldheim Publishers, Ltd.

Hoerr, Thomas R. (2000). *Becoming a Multiple Intelligences School*. Alexandria, VA: Association for Supervision and Curriculum Development.

Horowitz, Rabbi Yakov. (2008). *Living and Parenting: A Down-to-Earth Guide*. Brooklyn, NY: Mesorah Publications, Ltd.

In the Garden of the Torah. (1994). Vol. I. Brooklyn, N.Y.: Sichos in English.

Klein, Rabbi Shmuel Yaakov. (2001). *To Teach a Jew*. Southfield, MI: Targum Press.

Kohn, Alfie. (1986). *No Contest: The Case Against Competition*. Boston: Houghton Mifflin Company.

_____. (1998). *What to Look For in a Classroom…and Other Essays*. San Francisco, CA: Jossey-Bass.

_____. (1999). *The Schools Our Children Deserve: Moving Beyond Traditional Classrooms and "Tougher Standards."* Boston and New York: Houghton Mifflin Company.

Lillard, Angeline. (March 2004). "Testing Mania." *Parenting for a New World*, Vol.XIII, No. 1, AMI-USA.

_____. (2005). *Montessori: The Science Behind the Genius*. New York, NY: Oxford University Press.

Paley, Vivian Gussin. (1993). *You Can't Say You Can't Play*. Cambridge, MA, and London, England: Harvard University Press.

_____. (1999). *The Kindness of Children*. Cambridge, MA, and London, England: Harvard University Press.

Palmer, Parker. (1998). *The Courage to Teach: Exploring the Inner Landscape of a Teacher's Life*. San Francisco, CA: Jossey-Bass, a Wiley Company.

Schneerson, Rabbi Menachem M. (1980). *Likkutei Sichot*, Vol. I, Bereishit. Brooklyn, NY: Kehot Publication Society.

_____. (1983). *Likkutei Sichot*, Vol. II, Shemot. Brooklyn, NY: Kehot Publication Society.

_____. (1999). *Likkutei Sichot*, Vol. V, Devarim. Brooklyn, NY: Vaad L'Hafotzas Sichos.

Tomlinson, Carol Ann. (2003). *Fulfilling the Promise of the Differentiated Classroom*. Alexandria, VA: Association for Supervision and Curriculum Development.

Tomlinson, Carol Ann, and McTighe, Jay. (2006). *Integrating Differentiated Instruction and Understanding by Design*. Alexandria, VA: Association for Supervision and Curriculum Development.

Touger, Rabbi Eliyahu. (1994). *In the Paths of Our Fathers*. Brooklyn, NY: Kehot Publication Society.

_____. (1995). *In the Garden of the Torah*. Vol. II. Brooklyn, NY: Sichos in English.

Willingham, Daniel T. (2009). *Why Don't Students Like School?* San Francisco, CA: Jossey-Bass, a Wiley Imprint.

Other Resources

Information Services, Association for Supervision and Curriculum Development
1703 North Beauregard Street
Alexandria, VA 22311-1714
Website: www.ascd.org
E-mail: member@ascd.org
ASCD Service Center – 1-800-933-2723
or 703-578-9600, then press 2

Two videos available from ASCD:
A Visit to a Differentiated Classroom
Instructional Strategies for the Differentiated Classroom

Understanding by Design Exchange website:
http://ubdexchange.org

Acknowledgments

Thank You ...

Mary Thurlow, who allowed me to use the DeKalb Professional Library at the Jim Cherry Teacher Center in Atlanta.

Philip Silverman, who read my manuscript and provided valuable feedback and more books to read.

Dawn Kreisberg for many conversations and the book by Tomlinson and McTighe.

Bev Fermon for even more material to read and for urging me to finish this book.

Rabbi Nochem Kaplan, Rabbi Emanuel Feldman, Rabbi Ariel and Michele Asa, Ruby Grossblatt, Rick Halpern, Dr. Sharon Habif, Dr. Leah Scheier, Bev Lewyn, Sidney and Linda Rothschild, and Ezra and Nechama Carter for their suggestions and encouragement.

Rivki Neuberger, Kathy Poodiack, and Avraham and Tamar Warga for their part in helping to find my publisher.

I am grateful for the dialogue that ensued with all of these friends and the opportunity they gave me to clarify my thoughts.

Most of all, thank you to my students, who opened up their hearts and let me in. They are the ones peeking out between the lines of this book and standing by me at every step of its writing.

SC

CPSIA information can be obtained at www.ICGtesting.com
Printed in the USA
244323LV00001B/4/P